THE GREAT GENERALS SERIES

This distinguished new series features the lives of eminent military leaders who changed history in the United States and abroad. Top military historians write concise but comprehensive biographies including the personal lives, battles, strategies, and legacies of these great generals, with the aim to provide background and insight into today's armies and wars. These books are of interest to the military history buff, and, thanks to fast-paced narratives and references to current affairs, they are also accessible to the general reader.

Patton by Alan Axelrod

Grant by John Mosier

Eisenhower by John Wukovits

LeMay by Barrett Tillman

MacArthur by Richard B. Frank

Stonewall Jackson by Donald A. Davis

Bradley by Alan Axelrod

Pershing by Jim Lacey

Andrew Jackson by Robert V. Remini

Sherman by Steven E. Woodworth

Washington by Gerald M. Carbone

Marshall by H. Paul Jeffers

Custer by Duane Schultz

Robert E. Lee

Lessons in Leadership

Noah Andre Trudeau

Foreword by General Wesley K. Clark

ROBERT E. LEE
Copyright © Noah Andre Trudeau, 2009.
All rights reserved.

First published in hardcover in 2009 by PALGRAVE MACMILLAN® in the
US—a division of St. Martin's Press LLC, 175 Fifth Avenue, New York, NY
10010.

Where this book is distributed in the UK, Europe and the rest of the world,
this is by Palgrave Macmillan, a division of Macmillan Publishers Limited,
registered in England, company number 785998, of Houndmills, Basingstoke,
Hampshire RG21 6XS.

Palgrave Macmillan is the global academic imprint of the above companies
and has companies and representatives throughout the world.

Palgrave® and Macmillan® are registered trademarks in the United States, the
United Kingdom, Europe and other countries.

ISBN: 978-0-230-10344-3

Library of Congress Cataloging-in-Publication Data is available from the
Library of Congress.

A catalogue record of the book is available from the British Library.

Design by Letra Libre

First PALGRAVE MACMILLAN paperback edition: October 2010

10 9 8 7 6 5 4 3 2 1

Printed in the United States of America.

Contents

Foreword

General Robert E. Lee, noblest son of the South, destined from his first days at West Point for greatness, was the tragic hero of a lost war. For those of us of a certain age and from parts of the United States, he is the first general we ever learned of, the most important general we ever discussed in school, and a leader we strove to emulate. To some, Lee's is a familiar story, glorified once again each February in schools and newspaper editorials across the South. To others, why a losing general in a lost cause should be so revered remains a bit of a mystery.

The answers, and a few necessary correctives, are here, in Noah Andre Trudeau's sparkling biography. He cuts to the core of Lee, his background, contributions, strengths, weaknesses, and failures. And in so doing, he shines a strong light on both the terrible conflict that divided our nation as well as many of the sectional political issues that have cast a long shadow in American politics.

Lee certainly came from good stock. His father was a Revolutionary War hero, and his mother stemmed from one of Virginia's top families. As Trudeau tells it, Lee was brought up with a doting and dependent mother who compensated for an absentee, famous father. His upbringing, his natural talents, and his excellent early education, all combined to make him stand out at West Point. He graduated in the class of 1829 with high academic standing and the high esteem of his classmates. He was commissioned into the Corps of Engineers.

+━◇━+

Excellence at West Point is not necessarily an accurate indicator of future accomplishments. But in Lee's case, his achievements there, and especially his character and bearing, accurately foretold a brilliant career. As a young engineer, he was given independent responsibilities and leadership which might not have gone to an infantryman or artillerist. His eye for terrain and his natural disposition to bold action earned him a brilliant reputation as the young captain who opened the way for the General Winfield Scott's successful campaign into the heart of Mexico. With his participation in the highest councils of war, Lee no doubt honed an interest and instinct for strategy that would make him a formidable opponent to a series of Union leaders.

At the end of the Mexican War, a still youthful Lee went on to achieve all the successes a small Army could bestow—the Superintendency of the Military Academy at West Point, and the transfer to the "command track" with service as deputy commander of the U.S. 2nd Cavalry Regiment and then command of the U.S. Army's 2nd Cavalry on the Texas frontier in the late 1850's.

Somehow, Lee juggled all this military achievement with a vibrant family life. He courted and married Mary Custis, a descendant of George Washington's wife, Martha, and a member of an even more illustrious Virginia family. He and Mary raised seven children; by all reports their life was happy and adoring. Fame, success, family, social prestige—no officer could have asked for more.

Then, the tragedy of America's fateful reckoning with sectionalism and slavery intervened. Lee was confronted personally and profoundly with perhaps the deepest conflict that could affect a soldier—loyalty to his country and his Army, versus loyalty to his state, family, and home. And it was Lee's character in facing, choosing, and living through the consequences of this terrible dilemma that has so elevated him in the annals of American history.

†➤═➤═◄†

Trudeau tells the vivid story of the battles—the terrible, bloody struggle at Antietam (where Lee's plans were captured before the battle by the Union), Lee's effort behind Stonewall Jackson's Shenandoah Valley Campaign, the decisive defeat of the Union forces at Chancellorsville, the tragedy at Gettysburg, and on the final, soulful ending at Appomattox Courthouse. This is as clear and as gripping a recounting as has ever been written.

But even more importantly, Trudeau takes us behind the battles into Lee's relationships, gestures, moods, and style. Lee was actually offered the command of the Union forces—perhaps not surprisingly since his patron, Winfield Scott, was still ensconced as the President's military advisor. Instead, Lee resigned from the U.S. Army, and accepted his duty as military advisor to Confederate President Jefferson Davis (himself a West Pointer, and former U.S. Secretary of War and a contemporary of Lee's). He gained Davis's trust and confidence sufficiently to enable him to have a relatively free hand in the strategy of the war in the critical northern Virginia area at some crucial times. Trudeau chronicles Lee's relationships with Jackson, Longstreet, and Beauregard—relationships that were vital, and sometimes challenging and difficult.

Most valuable are the tantalizing glimpses into Lee's character in this book. Retreat, withdrawal, and defeat are the toughest military operations, and are particularly difficult from an emotional perspective for leaders. Great commanders in the offensive have often buckled and failed in the retrograde. And for Lee, the consequences were the most profound of all, for as he well realized, his failure to win against the Union Army at Gettysburg consigned the Confederacy first to remaining indefinitely on the strategic defensive, and ultimately to defeat.

Notwithstanding these circumstances, Lee continued to lead, to inspire, and to take substantial personal risks. Exhaustion and failing health never extinguished his offensive mindset or his dedication to his troops. The vignettes of his courage and his humanity are numerous, and have contributed greatly to his legendary status. He finished the war admired, and loved, more so even than the cause and men he served.

Lee left no memoir. And after Antietam, he seldom revealed in writing his innermost plans and thoughts. He clearly made mistakes and misjudgments that, as is usually the case, were reflected in the outcomes of his battles. In the service of an ambitious president, he never gained the scope of command or the freedom of action that his talents and qualities warranted. In the end, his was dedicated service for what he may even have known at the outset was a lost cause and, increasingly, a cause that was seen to be both immoral and unworthy.

All of this is the stuff of heroic and tragic legend. Trudeau's outstanding biography brings Lee to life for another generation of Americans who seek to grasp the tragedy and honor of the South and its struggle against a stronger union, and to reflect once again on the trials and travails of great generalship.

—*General Wesley K. Clark*

Beginnings, Endings

There are few figures of the American Civil War who hold a place of such reverence and importance as Robert E. Lee of Virginia. Viewed from the comfortable distance of time, his life is often reduced to its simplest components—duty and honor, with more than a touch of military audacity. Yet from the moment he rode onto history's center stage, until he left it, he undertook a profound and seldom-acknowledged personal journey. It began and ended in Virginia, marking moments of exceptionally dramatic turning points for Lee and America.

June 1, 1862

General Robert E. Lee, newly appointed commander of the Army of Northern Virginia, departed Richmond around 1:00 P.M. accompanied by a few aides and orderlies. They rode east to the Nine

Mile Road and followed it. As they did so they passed through some of the human debris of a battle that had taken place on May 31 near a once-picturesque road intersection called Seven Pines. Under the overall command of General Joseph E. Johnston, some 20,000 Rebel soldiers had attacked a smaller Federal force holding an advanced position. At the end of the bloody day, more than 5,000 Rebels were casualties and very little had been gained. Counted among the fallen was General Johnston, whose wound was serious enough to force him to leave the field. His immediate successor in the army's chain of command quickly made it evident that he was in over his head and incapable of directing the substantial force the Confederacy had assembled to protect its capital. Later that day, Lee received a note from Confederate President Jefferson Davis which explained that Johnston was wounded and that Lee would succeed the fallen officer in command of the army.

It was a daunting, even impossible assignment. A massive U.S. army had marched and bulled its way up the Virginia Peninsula to within a few miles of Richmond. Some efforts had delayed the enemy advance, but not once was a serious blow struck. Seven Pines was supposed to change that, but at the end of the day there was scant to show for all the blood spent. The task of turning things around had been given to Lee.

He was ready. All his life, it seemed, had been leading to this moment. All his military skill, experience, leadership, and intuition would be needed if the nascent nation was to survive the next weeks. A staffer with the party pointed out the Hughes home, then serving as army headquarters. In just a few minutes, Lee would formally take command of the forces defending Richmond.

Robert E. Lee and his staff drew up before the humble house and dismounted. Soon it would be all his responsibility to find a way to fight for peace.

April 9, 1865

General Robert E. Lee looked deep into the darkness of a military field commander's worst nightmare. His once magnificent army had been cruelly whittled to a division's size by battle losses, disease, and desertion. Ahead and behind him was the enemy, determined and in great strength. To one side an impassible river, to the other rough country unfit for large numbers of men moving in formation. No training or experience ever prepares a soldier for the prospect of capitulation. Speaking with one of several staff officers and senior subordinates this day, Lee cut to the sharp edge of the matter: "The question is, is it right to surrender this army. If it is right, then *I* will take *all* the responsibility."[1]

Lee had carefully dressed in a new uniform that morning, including, as another officer present recollected, "sword and sash and an embroidered belt, boots, and gold spurs."[2] A number of messages had already passed between the lines, trying to pin down the details for a meeting with the enemy commander, Lieutenant General Ulysses S. ("Unconditional Surrender") Grant. As each update arrived, Lee invariably queried the dispatch bearer for his opinion of how matters stood. Lee's principal subcommander, Lieutenant General James Longstreet, was characteristically blunt. "I asked if the bloody sacrifice of his army could in any way help the cause in other quarters," the officer remembered. "He thought not. Then, I said, your situation speaks for itself."[3]

The sun had eased past the meridian when at last a note came from Grant himself, acknowledging Lee's previous efforts to communicate his intentions, indicating his present course of travel, and deferring to the Rebel chieftain to select the meeting place. Some little details were settled and then it was time to go. Just a few hours earlier, when any hope of extracting the army from its dilemma had been extinguished, Lee confided to an aide: "Then there is nothing left [for] me to do but to go and see General Grant, and I would rather die a thousand deaths."[4]

Accompanied only by one staff officer, a courier, and a Union liaison, Lee began the slow ride down the hill to the village of Appomattox Court House, where he would surrender the Army of Northern Virginia.

First he would make peace and then, perhaps, find peace.

CHAPTER 1

A First Family of Virginia

There was military glory in Robert E. Lee's makeup, along with conflicting impulses of responsibility and recklessness, determination and overconfidence, integrity and duplicity, and honorable behavior and imprudence. Not in conflict were leadership, charisma, and a constant fear of failure. Most of the dark side came from his father, Henry Lee III, known, thanks to his mounted exploits during the Revolutionary War, as "Light Horse Harry." Harry Lee was a widower and governor of Virginia when he met and courted Miss Ann Hill Carter, whose family controlled 25,000 choice acres along the James River below Richmond. He was thirty-seven and she twenty. Everyone hoped that fame and fortune had been joined; what no one expected was that ahead of these newlyweds was a life of disappointment, separation, and broken promises.

Harry Lee was both unlucky and unwise. It was expected that he would live in a manner suited to a genuine war hero and offspring of one of the FFVs (First Families of Virginia). This he attempted to do through a series of investments that promised high returns but only delivered red ink. Instead of chasing foxes, Harry Lee found himself dodging creditors, even spending time in jail when he ran out of running room. Public knowledge of his failings was made evident when first Ann's father and then several of her wealthy relatives arranged their wills so that she—and not husband Harry—would have access to Carter family wealth.

Still, the evidence is that Ann was devoted to Harry, who was faithful to her. He brought three children with him from a previous marriage; his union with Ann Carter would eventually add six more. The fifth came along on January 19, 1807. For his name Ann turned to those of two of her favorite brothers—Robert and Edward Carter.

Robert Edward Lee was all of six years old when Harry Lee left the family for the Caribbean in search of better prospects, never to return. The father kept in touch through a series of letters to Ann's oldest son, Charles Carter Lee. In one of these notes is preserved the first written mention of child number five. "Robert was always good," Harry informed Charles, "and will be confirmed in his happy turn of mind by his ever watchful and affectionate mother."[1]

When news of Harry Lee's death reached Ann and the kids (Robert was eleven) the family was living in northern Virginia. In time the dead father's shadow would touch Robert Edward with a strange affection. Near the end of his own life, with many clamoring for him to write his memoirs of tumultuous times, Robert Edward Lee instead threw himself into editing a new edition of his father's *Memoirs of the War in the Southern Department of the United States*. Noticeably missing from the son's précis of his father's life were any of the social embarrassments or financial distresses that forced Ann (raised in a world of sheltered leisure) to manage her own household with a constant eye on the bottom line.

With his father gone, and his two older brothers settled into career tracks away from the family's home in Alexandria, Virginia, Robert Edward became the man of the house. His already close-knit ties with his mother grew even closer, especially as he nursed the increasingly frail Ann through periods of sickness. In the process something of her own strong faith and acceptance of God's will transferred to her son-caregiver. In later life, when a particular stratagem either succeeded or failed, Lee would quickly get past any emotional baggage with the observation that it was all God's will.

Somehow Robert Edward found the time for his education—first with a tutor at his aunt's estate, then in the newly established Alexandria Academy. Another small piece of the Lee trail emerged from this period in the form of an evaluation by one of his academy teachers, William B. Leary. "In the various branches, to which his attention has been applied, I flatter myself that his information will be found adequate to the most sanguine expectations of his friends," wrote Leary. "With me he has read all the minor classics, in addition to Homer and Longinus, Tacitus and Cicero. He is well versed in arithmetic, Algebra and Euclid."[2]

At the time of his sixteenth birthday, it became incumbent on Robert Edward to seek a career. Modest family finances and one brother just through college ruled out that avenue. Because of his father's bad choices and indebtedness, there was no plantation to manage. However, thanks to his father's notable military record there was a built-in recommendation for a Lee to attend West Point. Robert Edward never explained why he settled on that course. Emory Thomas summarizes the consensus of Lee biographers with the observation that "no one can know how enthusiastic Robert was or was not at the time."[3]

Even though he was Harry Lee's son, it was not a given that Robert Edward would be accepted, so his family took care to pull every string. Congressman R. S. Garnett invoked Light Horse Harry and insisted that the young Lee "has strong hereditary claims on the country." From older brother and lawyer Charles Carter Lee came assurances that "his disposition is amiable, & his morals irreproachable."[4] A letter finally arrived for Robert Edward from Secretary of War John C. Calhoun, containing good and bad news. The good was that young Lee had been accepted to West Point; the bad was that because of the very large number of applicants he could not be admitted until July 1, 1825—a year's delay.

In confirming his acceptance, Robert E. Lee emerges from the shadows with the first letter known to be in his handwriting:

Sir

I hereby accept the appointment to the station of a Cadet in the service of the United States, with which I have been honnoured [*sic*] by the President.

The above is the declaration of consent which my letter of appointment instructs me should accompany my acceptance.

I remain with the highest respect, Sir

Your most obliged & most obedient servant

R.E. Lee[5]

CHAPTER 2

West Point

West Point in 1825 was a specialty school with an emphasis on engineering. Courses in science and mathematics dominated the curriculum, with the military arts (formation drills, basic tactics, and strategic planning) coming in a distant second. The one foreign language required of the students was French, the language of the most important texts of military science and engineering. Even though most West Point graduates of the time could not speak or write French, almost all could read it.

Since an officer in the field might well be expected to produce accurate topographic sketches, another associated discipline that found its way onto Lee's schedule was freehand drawing, with an emphasis on the human figure. The good-humored Frenchman who taught the course assured his class (all sophomores) that anyone could master the art. "There are only two lines in drawing, the straight line and the curve line," he proclaimed. "Every one can draw a straight line and every one can draw a curve line—therefore every one can draw."[1]

Missing from the various courses of instruction, routines, and ceremonies that took place on the campus was anything to engender a special allegiance to the United States of America. This had nothing to do with regional political pressures or biases, and everything to do with the fact that in 1825 the United States of America was very much a work in progress that had yet to transcend sectional boundaries. More than one Lee biographer has pointed out that a law textbook in limited circulation while Lee was matriculating agreed with the contention that the individual states had a constitutional right of secession. There's no evidence that Lee ever saw this textbook; however, it can't be ruled out that such ideas circulated in the general conversation. As a distinguished American statesman would observe some thirty-six years in the future, the Union at this time "was a sentiment, but not much more."[2]

It was into this environment that Robert E. Lee arrived in June 1825, just one member in an entry class numbering 107. The students were first assigned to tents that had been erected on a plain known as Camp Adams. Each cadet was subjected to an oral entrance exam and something of his character was also evaluated. The eighty who passed this initial screening received rooms in the stone dormitories called the North and South Barracks. Just to the west of the South Barracks was the two-story academic building where most of the classes were held. Add a mess hall and the world that would be home to Robert E. Lee for the next four years was complete.

For the rest of that first summer, the plebes (eventually joined by their upperclassmen) were put through military drills and learned the code of behavior expected of gentlemen at West Point.

It was the good fortune of this entry class of 1825 that they arrived in the midst of the tenure of superintendent Lieutenant Colonel Sylvanus Thayer. Himself a graduate and a veteran of the War of 1812, Thayer had been brought in to upgrade the school in 1817. During his term, standards of instruction improved and discipline became a watchword. Even though the basic teaching format was rote memory, there is little doubt that the young men who completed the four years emerged extremely well-schooled in the military arts.

All that could be said of Lee up until this time was that he fit in. There was nothing in his demeanor that marked him as any different from any of the other civilians beginning the process of becoming soldiers. That soon began to change. Lee showed himself to be a superior student by finishing his initial term standing third in his class. Equally impressive, his demerit count (issued for rule infractions) stood at zero. As a result he was named a cadet staff sergeant, a singular honor for a first-year man. Lee's academic performance for his sophomore year was equally impressive and he ranked second this time around with the demerit count still zero. Thanks to these accomplishments, Lee was allowed a furlough—his first opportunity to visit home in two years.

There was a bittersweet quality to his family reunion. His mother's health, never the best, had, if anything, worsened. Nevertheless, she made a number of family visits with her son, whose spiffy cadet uniform caught the admiring eyes of several female cousins, one of whom later wrote of Lee's "manly beauty and attractiveness of manner."[3] It was during a visit to the home of Edward Carter Turner in Fauquier County (Ann Lee's extended family) that Robert renewed his acquaintance with his cousin Mary from Arlington.

Mary Anne Randolph Custis was the only surviving child of George Washington Parke Custis, Martha Washington's grandson and the adopted son of George Washington. Accounts of her at this time describe a young woman whose slight frailty and modest beauty were more than offset by her vivaciousness, wit, and intelligence. There's no evidence of any special attraction between Robert and Mary, but that would soon change. Lee's furlough ended much too quickly and he returned to West Point.

Once again hard work paid off. Lee ended the season ranked number two, for which he received appointment as cadet adjutant, the highest status for a student. It was in his fourth and final year that Lee and his classmates were given a course in military engineering. Taught under that heading were lessons in temporary field fortifications, permanent fortifications, artillery science, grand tactical, as well as civil and military architecture. When this season came to a close, Lee, still second in his class, saw his name published on a special list of distinguished cadets. This in turn entitled him the right to select the branch of service he wanted for his first assignments. Lee chose the Engineer Corps.

The young man who graduated West Point in 1829 had yet to reveal the qualities that later generations would indelibly associate with Robert E. Lee. That he was a superior student is clear. He also possessed what would today be termed strong people skills. A classmate—friend, fellow Virginian, and future Civil War general Joseph E. Johnston—declared that "no other youth or man so united the qualities that win warm friendship and command high respect. For he was full of sympathy and kindness, genial and fond of gay conversation, even fun, while his correctness of demeanor and attention to all duties, personal and official, and a dignity as much a part of himself as the eloquence of his person, gave him a superiority that every one acknowledged in his heart."[4] Other classmates, taking a more direct tack, dubbed Lee the "Marble Model" for his good looks and military bearing.

How all these attributes and all this practical knowledge would survive contact with the real world remained to be seen.

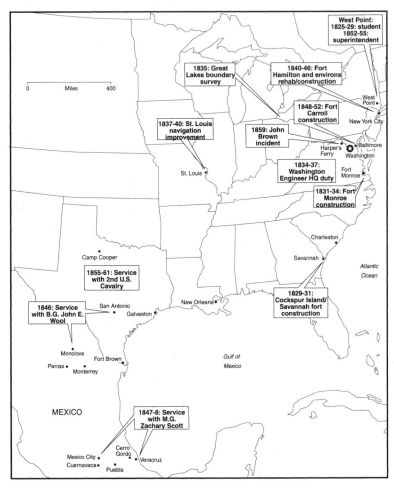

West Point:
1825-29: student
1852-55:
superintendent

1835: Great
Lakes boundary
survey

1840-46: Fort
Hamilton and environs
rehab/construction

1848-52: Fort
Carroll
construction

West
Point

1837-40: St. Louis
navigation
improvement

1859: John
Brown
incident

New York City

Baltimore

Harper's
Ferry   Washington

1834-37:
Washington
Engineer HQ duty

Fort
Monroe

St. Louis

1831-34: Fort
Monroe
construction

Charleston

Camp Cooper

Savannah

Atlantic
Ocean

1855-61: Service
with 2nd U.S.
Cavalry

1846: Service
with B.G. John E.
Wool

San Antonio

Galveston

New Orleans

1829-31:
Cockspur Island/
Savannah fort
construction

Monclova

Fort Brown

Parras

Monterrey

Gulf of
Mexico

MEXICO

1847-8: Service
with M.G.
Zachary Scott

Cerro
Gordo

Mexico City

Veracruz

Cuernavaca

Puebla

Miles   400

0

LEE AND THE U.S. ARMY: 1825–1861

CHAPTER 3

Engineer and Father

Immediately upon returning home, Robert E. Lee resumed his duties as caretaker for his fifty-six-year-old mother. Something she said when he first left home for West Point speaks to the deep relationship the two shared. "How can I live without Robert?" she asked, "He is both son and daughter to me."[1] This made her death, coming little more than a month after he arrived, especially painful. Many years later Lee would still recall the intimate details of her passing as if it had just taken place. While still awaiting his first engineer assignment, he assisted his older brother Carter in the settlement of their mother's estate. He also began his courtship of cousin Mary Custis, who was soon writing in her diary of the "worldly young gentleman who flattered my vanity & pleased me in spite of myself."[2] Then orders arrived directing U.S. Army Lieutenant Robert E. Lee to report to Savannah, Georgia.

This was the first in a succession of postings that eventually brought him to the attention of his superiors and marked him as a young officer to watch. It also began a pattern of assignments beset by delays and lack of funding, which often resulted in his moving on before the job was done. While in South Carolina (1829–31), he was involved in the difficult work of constructing a powerful masonry fortress (soon named Fort Pulaski) in the midst of a treacherous marsh fully exposed to the ravages of coastal storms. From late 1831 until late 1834, Fort Monroe on the tip of the Virginia Peninsula was Lee's assigned station. There he worked on rehabilitating rundown sections of the bastion and learned a bit about navigating the minefield of conflicting lines of authority: the engineers versus the infantry/artillery.

For three years (1834–37) Lee was in Washington as assistant to the chief of the Engineer Department. It was not an especially challenging job; when he wasn't chasing after distant project managers to clear up their bookkeeping, Lee was experiencing firsthand how the power of patronage could skew choice assignments away from the most talented. Then, in 1837, Lee was sent to Missouri, where the fickle Mississippi River was slowly but surely silting up the river port of St. Louis. Although not trained in fluid mechanics, Lee devised an ingenious, practical, and cost-effective scheme that utilized a series of man-made dikes built mid-stream to redirect the river current. These changes accomplished the hard work of scouring the St. Louis port basin and reopening the passageway for business traffic. At the same time some of his crews were blasting a channel through a series of rapids upstream to facilitate shipping movement. Neither job had been completed when Lee was moved again in 1840 to the New York City area, though his accomplishments were sufficient to merit promotion to captain.

From his headquarters in Fort Hamilton, Lee directed work on four military installations under construction in the area of today's Verrazano Narrows Bridge. These tasks kept him busy through

1846. During this period Lee acquired confidence in his ability to solve complicated problems, showed a willingness to—in contemporary parlance—think outside the box, and further polished his growing reputation within the army.

Overlaying all this professional activity was his personal life. On June 30, 1831, Lee married Mary Custis of Arlington and began a lifelong relationship with the woman he sometimes called Molly or Mana. They were a study of contrasts. He was vigorous, robust in health, well-organized, routine oriented, and thrifty. She was verging on indolent, often sickly, usually disorganized, unpredictable, and used to a life where little was denied her. They were apart more often than together—he at some distant post, she often forsaking their *maison de jour* for the comforts of the Custis family mansion in Arlington. Yet there is no evidence that either ever sought release from the other.

It was a family blessed with children: George Washington Custis Lee in 1832, Mary Lee in 1835, William Henry Fitzhugh Lee ("Rooney" to most, though Lee himself preferred "Fitzhugh") in 1837, Anne Carter Lee in 1839, Eleanor Agnes Lee in 1841, Robert E. Lee Jr. in 1843, and Mildred Childe Lee in 1846. For his part, Lee was an attentive and dutiful, if often physically distant, head of the family. He corresponded with all his children and his letters reveal a mingling of stern responsibility with warm affection not often associated with the later figure of statues and portraits.

"He was always bright and gay with us little folk," recollected Robert Jr. of the good times, "playing and joking with us."[3] However, Robert Sr. enforced a demanding code of behavior on his children that by modern standards would be considered obsessive. "You must do all in your power to save me pain," he constantly reminded his boys.[4] Some of his children were granted playful nicknames (first-born George was "Boo," first daughter Mary was "Daughter," Eleanor Agnes was "Wigs," Robert Jr. sometimes "Brutus," and last to arrive Mildred "Precious Life"), and all received continual long-distance advice. "You must expect discomforts and annoyances all through life," he counseled Eleanor Agnes in one note. "No place or position is secure from them, and you must make up your mind to meet with them and bear them."[5]

Raised largely by his mother, Lee was thoroughly comfortable in the company of other women—to the point where a more skeptical modern observer might well assume intimate liaisons occurred where none existed. Not long after his marriage, Lee learned that Miss Eliza Mackay of Savannah, a dark-eyed beauty who had won his heart, was herself to be wed. Writing her right after he learned the news, Lee declared "I have been in tears ever since the thought of *losing* you."[6] Another special friend was "Markie" Williams, great-granddaughter of Martha Washington. "Did you not feel your cheeks *pale* when I was so near you?" Lee wondered on one occasion. "Oh Markie, Markie, when will you ripen?" he chided on another.[7] His at times intimate and at times innocently flirtatious relationships with some female acquaintances represent a fascinating and little-known part of his personality, which was about to take on the character of a warrior.

Barely six months after the birth of his last child, Lee received orders that would change his life. He was to join the engineering staff with U.S. forces in Texas, who were engaged in operations against Mexican forces along the Rio Grande.

Robert E. Lee was going to war.

CHAPTER 4

Mexico

After closing his affairs in New York and making out his will, Lee traveled by steamer to New Orleans (carrying $60,000 in government funds entrusted to his care), next by transport ship to Port Lavaca on the Texas coast some 120 miles south of Galveston, then overland to San Antonio. There he reported for duty with Brigadier General John E. Wool. Four days after his arrival, Lee was part of an engineer scouting detail sent to locate the best line of march southward for Wool's 1,400 soldiers. It was his first operation against an armed enemy.

For the next eleven days the engineers labored constantly to smooth out rough road patches and to bridge small streams, making it possible for the main column to cover 164 miles without serious incident. There was a pause at the Rio Grande while the engineers put together a pontoon bridge and constructed defensive earthworks to help secure the advanced position. Lee, reporting at this time to Captain William D. Fraser, evidently had his hand in just about everything.

About 150 miles to the south, another American expeditionary force under Brevet Brigadier General Zachary Taylor had taken the fortress city of Monterrey and entered into a truce with the Mexican command in the general area. That agreement included Wool's column, which halted at Monclova, securing the western approaches to Monterrey. Lee was kept busy drafting maps and identifying defensive positions. General Wool (called "Old Fussy" by his men) was impressed enough by the Virginia engineer officer's attention to detail that he included him in his planning meetings.

Already Lee was displaying elements of the aggressiveness that would so mark his mature career. He was among those who believed that the truce was a mistake, coming as it did after a major Mexican defeat at Monterrey. Writing to his wife, Lee was adamant that "advantage should have been taken of our success, & perhaps the whole Mexican Army would have fallen into our hands."[1]

As soon as the truce ended without any larger agreement, Wool had his column marching southward to the village of Parras, which controlled one of the major roads that would be critical to the enemy in any counteroffensive movement. Lee's actions included clearing passages for wagon use and scouting possible routes. Christmas found him near Parras. Writing on Christmas Eve to his distant sons Custis and Fitzhugh, Lee assured them, "if I had one of you on each side of me riding on ponies, such as I could get you, I would be comparatively happy."[2]

In the larger scheme of things, U.S. operations in northern Mexico were winding down. If camp rumor was to be believed, the focus of the war was about to shift to the Mexican coast, with U.S. forces under Major General Winfield Scott poised to land at Veracruz, Mexico's principal Gulf port. Much to Lee's surprise, orders arrived on January 16, 1847, directing him to report to Scott's headquarters at Brazos Santiago, at the mouth of the Rio Grande.

The decision to transfer Lee appears to have come from Scott's chief of engineers, Colonel Joseph G. Totten. As head of the engineer bureau in Washington, it had been Totten who had sent Lee off on many of his assignments, and who had read the reports of his fine field work. The two had worked side by side for brief periods when Lee was operating out of the Washington office and Totten had formed a positive opinion of the young officer, so when Scott began organizing for the next campaign, Totten used his clout to bring his promising colleague into the operation.

Thanks to this friend in a high place, and the small number of engineers attached to the general staff, Lee found himself part of the select group that Scott considered his "little cabinet." Beyond anything specific in terms of strategies or tactics, Lee was given invaluable insight to the processes by which major military decisions were made and implemented.

On March 9, 1847, U.S. troops landed on Collada Beach just south of Veracruz against weak opposition. Two days earlier, Lee had been with Scott and the rest of his staff aboard a small ship investigating possible landing sites. The craft came near enough to the Mexican fort of San Juan de Ulua to draw some heavy-caliber shells, all of which missed. Included in the entourage with Lee were a future battlefield adversary, George Gordon Meade, and future peers Joseph E. Johnston and P. G. T. Beauregard.

Scott's first decision upon coming ashore was whether to take the citadel city by siege or storm. The engineers unanimously opted for siege and Scott concurred. As one of Scott's leading engineers, Lee was employed siting battery locations, laying out lines of investment, and directing construction. Models and diagrams seen only on West Point chalk boards now rose out of the Mexican soil.

Lee's job was not without its dangers. On March 19, entering a section of the American front lines at dusk, he was fired on by a nervous U.S. sentry, the bullet passing between his left arm and body. As Lee's preeminent biographer, Douglas Southall Freeman, dryly observed: "A deviation of a fraction of an inch in the soldier's aim would have changed some very important chapters in the history of the United States."[3] A more pleasant occasion happened soon after this when Robert Edward encountered his brother, Sidney Smith Lee, who commanded a naval artillery piece assigned to one of the siege batteries.

Scott's siege of Veracruz came to a successful conclusion on March 29 when the city's garrison surrendered. In a reorganization of staff positions that took place immediately afterward, Colonel Totten returned to Washington, making Lee the second ranking engineer officer on the scene. It was clear, too, that he had favorably impressed General Scott, who mentioned him by name in orders.

The capture of Veracruz was a double-edged victory for Winfield Scott. On the one hand, it provided him a secure supply base, easily accessible to U.S. shipping in the Gulf. On the other, its location in the tropical coastal region made it a dangerous place to linger when the summer season arrived with yellow fever, the dreaded vomito. Scott's only recourse was to push on for the interior. He decided to follow the National Highway, which wriggled to the northwest through a chain of ridges and hills that offered plenty of defensive opportunities to an active enemy.

Thanks to a lack of sufficient numbers of animals to pull his supply wagons, Scott could only thrust inland with perhaps a quarter of his fighting force. Nevertheless, the 2,000-man column commanded by Brigadier General David E. Twiggs set off on April 8. By the evening of April 11, Twiggs had reached the foothills, where he learned that the Mexicans, under their charismatic leader Antonio Lopez de Santa Anna, had taken up strong defensive positions centered on a critical pass near the Cerro Gordo (Fat Hill) ranch. His chief engineer, P. G. T. Beauregard, scouted the enemy's left flank and reported a difficult but viable path. After assessing the possibilities, Twiggs decided to tackle Cerro Gordo head on. He issued orders for an April 14 assault, which he cancelled late on April 13 upon learning that General Scott was himself coming to the front.

Scott arrived around midday with his staff. Intrigued by the possible flanking route discovered by Beauregard (who had taken ill), Scott detailed Captain Robert E. Lee to fully determine the route's potential. Lee set off on the morning of April 15 accompanied by one guide named John Fitzwalter. In carrying out this reconnaissance, Lee demonstrated a trait that would mark his later generalship of Southern armies. His risk tolerance was in direct proportion to the importance of the assigned task. Since his scout had the real prospect of providing American forces with the chance to crack the Cerro Gordo position without a bloody frontal assault, Lee was prepared to accept high risks to complete the mission.

He went as far as Beauregard had and then further. He agreed with his colleague's assessment that with a little work, the trail could be used by a column of troops. Determined to probe it until he was assured it brought him around the enemy's flank, Lee and his increasingly reluctant guide pressed on. As last they reached a spring accessed by a path coming up from the south. Given the evidence of the heavy foot traffic he observed, Lee concluded he had indeed reached a point in rear of the enemy flank.

Suddenly, the sound of Spanish voices nearby warned of imminent danger. While his guide set out for home (other accounts have him hiding nearby), Lee tucked himself behind a large log close to the spring, well covered with brush. The sounds heralded the arrival of a squad of Mexican soldiers intent on filling their canteens. This first group was followed by another and another as the hours passed. At one point a Mexican stepped over the log, nearly treading on the concealed U.S. officer. Not until nightfall did the procession of thirsty soldiers come to an end, allowing Lee to return to the American lines.

Showing a high degree of confidence in his young engineer officer, Scott promptly dispatched details to clear the pathway blazed by Beauregard and Lee. The route was declared passable on the morning of April 17, the working parties had been undetected, and Scott had a flanking column in motion. The axiom about no plan surviving contact with the enemy proved itself again. Mexican soldiers were encountered in greater numbers than the picket line expected, a sharp engagement ensued (this day had been reserved for marching into position), and the flankers stalled.

General Scott, never losing sight of his objective, organized an attack for April 18. With the reinforced flanking force leading the way, U.S. forces captured Cerro Gordo after a day marked by times of hard fighting. Lee was with the flanking unit, and while not in the thick of the combat, saw enough to purge his thoughts of military glory. "You have no idea what a horrible sight a field of battle is," he said in a letter written a few days afterward to son Custis.[4]

Lee's courageous scout and his regular appearances where he was most needed brought special commendations from several field commanders. Even Winfield Scott was taken with all that he observed. Lee, he wrote in his report, was "indefatigable, during these operations, in reconnaissance as daring as laborious, and of the utmost value."[5] On August 24, Captain Lee was brevetted major, an honor that he learned of some time after the fact.

Scott's grand campaign was off to a strong start, but only that. A pursuit was kept up for just four miles, to the town of Jalapa, where everything came to a halt and the entire enterprise threatened to disintegrate. To maximize his offensive punch, Scott had used every man; consequently, the supply route back to Veracruz now swarmed with enemy irregulars making the journey possible only for heavily escorted trains. Then the one-year enlistments of many of his militia regiments began to expire and the majority of the citizen-soldiers professed their preference for the former designation over the latter. With nary a shot fired by the enemy, Scott's strength was whittled to 7,000 men. There was trouble, too, from the home front, where an unfriendly Polk administration (which viewed Scott as a potential rival in the next election) sorely vexed the army commander with its half measures, and saddled him with a plenipotentiary who bypassed Scott's authority and was empowered to negotiate a settlement without reference to the general. In this unhappy manner, three months passed with only a slight further advance to Puebla, Mexico's second largest city, 75 miles from the country's capital.

Winfield Scott now demonstrated a determined resolve, a willingness to find accommodation with civilian authorities, and a dedication to completing the mission that forcibly impressed those closest to him. Drills and discipline kept the army sharp despite its inaction, key reinforcements arrived, and Washington's man on the scene was turned into an ally. The advance was resumed; target: Mexico City.

Robert E. Lee continued to participate in Scott's strategy and planning sessions. One important project that he worked on was the preparation of maps showing the approaches to Mexico City. These were based on material Lee and Beauregard had discovered in the hacienda used by Santa Anna, supplemented by interviews with various travelers and merchants. Although inaccurate in some places and vague in others, they were sufficient to guide Scott in the next phase of his operation.

The American army (now increased to 14,000 strong) began departing Puebla on August 7, 1847, following the National Highway. Scott renewed his advance in the full knowledge that Santa Anna was concentrating every available Mexican soldier to defend the capital. Estimates suggested that the Americans would be outnumbered better than two to one, yet Scott never faltered. Five days later, "the once gorgeous seat of the Montezumas" (Scott's words) was in sight.[6] A Mexican strongpoint at El Penon was bypassed and the American advance shifted from the National

Highway (eastern approach) over to the Acapulco road (southern approach).

Mexico City was somewhat akin to an island, being fully encircled by a series of marshes that were crossed by highly exposed causeways. Further complicating the picture for Scott, and limiting his options, was a huge lava field, known as the pedregal that seemingly blocked access to avenues that promised an alternate axis of approach west of his current course. Scott needed to know if a way could be found to flank Santa Anna's new defenses at the Churubusco River sited to block the Acapulco road. He turned to Captain Lee.

Accompanied by the 11th U.S. Infantry and two companies of dragoons, Lee probed the pedregal wasteland, which one early historian described as a "raging sea of molten rock."[7] He determined that getting infantry across was possible, but the artillery would be another problem. After a hard day's effort, Lee returned to report that a trail sufficient to support the cannon could be managed and once through the pedregal there was a viable road that flanked the enemy's blocking position along the Churubusco River. That night, at another of his planning sessions, Scott put all the options on the table. One officer present was suitably impressed by Lee's report. "His talent for topography was peculiar, and he seemed to receive impressions intuitively, which it cost other men much labor to acquire," he commented afterward.[8]

Scott dismissed the conference without announcing a decision, but early the next day Lee was sent with the engineer company and 500 infantrymen to get the pedregal route fit for wagons. The task took until early afternoon, at which point the small column had broken out of the lava field and reached the flanking road Lee had identified. The soldiers also found Mexican soldiers present in strength. The fight that erupted, for the rest of this day at least, was principally an artillery exchange, with several of the American batteries firing from positions found for them by Captain Lee. Night fell before anything larger could develop, but it was clear to the U.S. commander on the scene that he was badly outnumbered. However, two engineers reported finding an unguarded ravine that led to the enemy rear, so a plan was hatched. Lee volunteered to carry it back across the inky black pedregal to General Scott.

Somehow Lee and his small escort picked their way across the hard stone pan scored with sharp-edged crevasses and reached Scott's headquarters—or at least where they had been when the day began. Dog-tired but determined, Lee continued his mission and at last reached the general's new location at 11:00 P.M. Himself anxious for news of the flanking party, Scott had sent out seven messengers, none of whom could navigate the stony wasteland. He now decided to hurry along some of the supporting columns he had pushed onto the trail opened by Lee. When the officers commanding these units professed concern about finding their way in the dark, Lee was pressed into service.

The plan called for these units to occupy the enemy's attention in front while the leading elements used the ravine to flank the position. When the officer in overall charge who was traveling with Lee pleaded exhaustion, Lee went forward to make certain that the soldiers were where they were supposed to be when they were supposed to be there. The resulting fight was a clear victory for the Americans, with the Mexicans withdrawing toward the Churubusco River line. U.S. forces closely pursued, following a route that skirted the western edge of the pedregal before turning onto a crossroad leading toward the east, hoping to cut off Santa Anna in his position blocking Scott's main body. In the fight that followed at Coyoacan, Lee was put in charge of a small force that waded the Churubusco River. The day's effort carried Scott's men to the very gates of Mexico City, though Santa Anna escaped the trap.

By the time the fighting had ended, Lee had been in the saddle and active for thirty-six hours. For his actions during those two days, the brevet major was advanced again to brevet lieutenant colonel. Looking back on what Lee had done, General Scott declared it "the greatest feat of physical and moral courage performed by any individual, in my knowledge."[9]

A truce signed on August 24 led nowhere, so active operations resumed on September 7. With his immediate superior on sick call, Lee now headed the engineer unit. A day's scouting by Lee and others provided Scott sufficient data to attack and overrun the strong outpost at Molino de Rey on September 8. Five days later, while feinting an attack from the south, Scott's main blow came from the west and overpowered the fortress of Chapultepec, allowing U.S. troops to press along two causeways to enter the city, forcing Santa Anna to evacuate.

Lee was a prominent part of the team of engineers who kept Scott current on enemy positions and avenues of approach. This time, his duties kept him on the move without sleep for forty-eight hours, so it should not be surprising that at the close of the battle of Chapultepec he collapsed in a faint.

A night's sleep proved sufficient and he was back in the saddle when a delegation from Mexico City surrendered the place to General Scott. In the aftermath of this great victory, Lee received his third brevet promotion to colonel. Ahead of him lay nine more months of service on this distant front, far from home. He now saw firsthand the negative aspects of political power when President Polk used some trumped-up charges to court martial General Scott, his presumed presidential rival, and relieve him of command. A rash of further court martials ensued as top officers fought among themselves for pieces of glory in the wake of the victory. On several occasions Lee was called to testify regarding what he had seen and done.

In twenty-one months of service in Mexico, Lee had learned much about himself and the process of commanding an army at war. His self-confidence was greatly strengthened knowing that he had not flinched while under fire. By remaining focused on the mission objective, Lee was able to exploit his physical stamina and to accept high risks for high returns. He also learned the values and pitfalls of a general's relationship with the civilian officials from whom all authority derived. When all was said and done, Robert E. Lee emerged from this conflict a confident and accomplished warrior.

On June 9, 1848, he departed Veracruz on the steamship *Portland*, heading for home.

CHAPTER 5

Toward the Abyss

When Lee arrived at his beloved Arlington on June 29 he found his family waiting to greet him. The nearly two-year absence had had its effects, as he discovered when he attempted to take Robert Jr. into his arms only to find he was hugging a neighbor's child; Robert Jr. would recall the moment many years later.[1] The army allowed Lee until September to catch up, then posted him to Baltimore, the family dutifully following. There he oversaw work on an addition to the harbor's defenses—Fort Carroll. While engaged in this project Lee had a bout with an undiagnosed fever, which some later writers identify as malaria.

In 1850 Lee saw his son Custis follow in his footsteps as a West Point cadet. Two years later, and much to his surprise, Lee followed Custis, reluctantly, as the newly designated superintendent of the military school on the Hudson. At that time the academy was overseen by the corps of engineers, which made sure that the man in charge was one of its own. Lee's assignment came from Colonel Totten, who simply ignored his appointee's half-hearted attempt to decline the honor. This appointment lasted all of three years. During his brief tenure, Lee was able to implement some modest disciplinary reforms and tried but failed to have the awkward cadet dress cap redesigned. He supervised several physical improvements to the campus (including a new riding stable) and made the cavalry training more realistic. While he saw no reason to tinker much with the curriculum, he did take seriously his obligation to keep a fatherly eye on the cadets. In one case he thought there was enough promise in one New York boy to liberally interpret the demerit rules to forestall a first-year dismissal. That young man, James McNeill Whistler, dropped out in his third year, but what was the army's loss proved a substantial gain for the world of painting.

Lee's checkout list from the West Point library at this time was heavy with French military histories and Napoleonic campaign studies. He also interacted with staff professor Dennis Hart Mahan, a strong advocate for using temporary field fortifications as part of any modern military strategy.

Then, in March 1855, Congress reacted to increasing clashes with western Native American tribes by adding four regiments (two infantry, two cavalry) to the U.S. Army roster. Secretary of War Jefferson Davis moved quickly to staff the newly authorized units and Lee became lieutenant colonel (second-in-line) of the 2nd U.S. Cavalry. For the first time in his twenty-six-year military career, Robert E. Lee would be in direct command of combat troops in the field.

This assignment took him first to St. Louis, then to northwest Texas, where he was posted to Camp Cooper, located between the Brazos and Colorado rivers. His immediate superior was Colonel Albert Sidney Johnston, said by many to be the very image of a soldier. (He was killed in action at Shiloh seven years later.)

Lee's duties were varied, much of them administrative. He was in the field on several occasions in pursuit of marauding bands, but more often was tied up helping adjudicate court martials. Life had settled into a busy if unchallenging routine when word came on October 21, 1857, that his wife's father, George Washington Parke Custis, had died. A request through channels granted him two months' leave and Lee was soon headed back to Arlington.

This proved to be the beginning of an exceptionally unhappy and unrewarding phase of his life, marked with leave extensions for nearly two years. He found his wife in a bad way, emotionally and physically, increasingly crippled by arthritis. His late father-in-law's estate was in even worse condition. Never well managed, it existed in a series of land parcels, each with its own problems. There was debt as well, perhaps as much as $10,000, and no one to pick up the reins save Lee himself. Included in the property now given into Lee's hands were a large number of slaves.

Lee's feelings toward the South's peculiar institution has generated much discussion over the years. He is on record saying, in an 1856 letter, that slavery was "a moral & political evil in any Country," a statement that, along with others of the same tenor, has led some to proclaim him anti-slavery in his sentiments.[2]

However, slavery was a reality in 1857 and the law of the land. Working hard to stabilize his father-in-law's estate and better his cash flow, Lee utilized the existing laws to his profit. When a number of Custis's slaves proved difficult to handle, Lee turned them over to a labor agent to farm them out. "Should you not be able to hire any or all of those people," Lee's instructions read, "you may dispose of them to the end of the year to the best advantage."[3] On another occasion, when a black couple of his were caught trying to escape north, Lee transferred them to lower Virginia, where there was less opportunity to repeat the attempt. He may well have believed that the day would come when slavery was no longer the law of the land, but that day was not in the 1850s.

He was able, to his credit, to improve the value of his late father-in-law's holdings to the point where the estate began to emerge from the red. The army cooperated by approving Lee's supplemental leave requests without argument. He was at his desk in Arlington poring over the estate books on the morning of October 17, 1859, when a young lieutenant named James Ewell Brown (shortened to "Jeb") Stuart arrived with a request for Lee to report at once to the War Department. There was trouble at Harper's Ferry, Virginia, where a band of armed men had entered the town and were inciting the local slaves to rebel against their masters.

Not waiting to even don his uniform, Lee hurried across the Potomac to the War Department, where he learned he was to be put in charge of a quick reaction force consisting of regulars from Fort Monroe, Maryland militiamen, and marines based at the Washington Navy Yard. The troops were assembling at Relay House, just outside Baltimore, on the B&O line. Lee hurried there accompanied by Stuart, who had volunteered as an aide. Riding the rails, Lee reached Harper's Ferry between 10:00 and 11:00 P.M. The marines and militiamen were with him, the regulars still in transit. Making a quick assessment of the situation, Lee telegraphed the regulars to return to Fort Monroe as he did not anticipate needing them.

No one had a clear idea of who was doing the invading. Whoever they were, they were barricaded in the thick-walled stone fire engine house and were holding hostages. Lee replaced the local vigilantes who had been besieging the engine house and established a secure perimeter. At first light, October 18, Lieutenant Stuart, under a flag of truce, delivered a message offering a safe surrender. He recognized the group's leader as the infamous John Brown of Kansas. Colonel Lee's offer was rejected, prompting a quickly mounted assault by the marines, who battered their way into the enclosure, capturing or killing all the rioters, as Lee called them. After securing the engine house and tending the wounded, Lee had the surviving rebels moved to Charlestown, Virginia, for trial.

His involvement in this affair would continue in December, when he was called to oversee security for Brown's execution, which took place in Charlestown on December 2. After another brief period to settle family affairs, on February 10, 1860, Lee was back on his way to Texas. His duties followed the same pattern as before, save that the larger national picture was dramatically deteriorating. The band-aids of compromise could no longer keep festering issues regarding slavery, states' rights, and the legality of secession from erupting. Lines were being drawn.

South Carolina threw down the gauntlet with an ordinance of secession, passed on December 20, 1860. On January 9, state troops fired on the steamer *Star of the West* in mid-harbor when it attempted to resupply the U.S. garrison holding Fort Sumter. Soon South Carolina was joined by Mississippi, Florida, Alabama, Georgia, and Louisiana. In early February, with Texas on the verge of seceding as well, Lee was summoned to report in person to the U.S. Army's general-in-chief, Winfield Scott, in Washington. His departure was briefly delayed in San Antonio, where state forces friendly to secession controlled the streets and were halting all U.S. soldiers. Lee was finally allowed to proceed.

Robert E. Lee's professional military life to this point had all been at the beck and call of the U.S. Army administration. He had gone where he had been ordered to go, and served without any public complaint. On the surface there could be no more loyal a public servant and soldier. Now that all began to change.

Lee returned to Arlington on March 1, 1861. Very soon afterward he had a closed-door meeting with General Scott. Neither man chose to recall the conversation, but obvious talking points would have been the increasingly unsettled conditions, the army's obligation to maintain order, and Lee's likely role in that process.

No decision about Lee's participation had been made when Lee departed.

In the South, the seceded states organized a government that, on March 15, tendered an offer to Lee to serve the newly christened Confederate States as a brigadier general. There is no evidence that he replied to this solicitation. The very next day the new president, Abraham Lincoln, promoted Lee to full colonel. He received the news on March 28 and formally accepted it two days later.

On April 12, South Carolina authorities in Charleston, fed up with the Fort Sumter stalemate, opened fire on the citadel, which surrendered the next day. Lincoln reacted by ordering a call-up of 75,000 militia to put down the growing insurrection. Then, on April 17, the state of Virginia signaled its firm resolve to withdraw from the Union. Lee was recalled to General Scott's office the next day. The same envelope that carried the general-in-chief's summons contained a note from one of Washington's powerful insiders, Francis P. Blair, asking Lee to visit him first.

Lee took both meetings on April 18. Blair, acting as Lincoln's surrogate, extended an offer to command all U.S. forces being organized to suppress the rebellion. According to Lee's 1868 recollection of the moment, "I declined the offer he made me to take command of the army that was to be brought into the field, stating as candidly and as courteously as I could, that though opposed to secession and depreciating war, I could take no part in an invasion of the Southern States."[4]

Lee repeated what he had said to General Scott, a fellow Virginian. Here again there is no credible record of what was said between the two. Scott likely expressed his deep regrets and, as a friend, pointed out to Lee that a prompt resignation would avoid the odium of resigning in the face of peremptory orders to take to the field.

Two days after these conversations, Lee submitted his formal letter of resignation from the U.S. Army. It was received on April 22 and officially accepted three days after that. On the same day his resignation reached the War Department, Lee was in Richmond meeting with Virginia's governor, John Letcher. When he emerged it was as a major general in the state militia, in charge of all land and naval forces. On the day Lee's resignation was officially accepted in Washington, Virginia provisionally joined the Confederacy, pending a popular referendum on the issue.

Lee's decision to take up arms against the U.S. Army is still the subject of much debate. His ostensible reason was a greater allegiance to his native Virginia, but the speed by which he passed from a soldier for Virginia to one for the Confederacy suggests that his state's decision to secede may have been the trigger to act but not the root cause.

Robert E. Lee was first and foremost a Southerner. His military service to that point had not created any supra-identification with the United States of America. His written references to the United States often refer to it in the plural sense. "I know of no other Country . . . ," he penned in 1857, "than the *United States* & their *Constitution*."[5] Efforts by Northern leaders to enforce a contrary will on the South deeply offended him. The South, he said in a letter written on January 23, 1861, justly "has been aggrieved by the acts of the North."[6] The flip side of Lee's profession to Francis Blair that he could not take part in an invasion of Southern states was that, as a Southerner, he could not abide it happening.

Also in the mix was a heritage deeply imbedded in Southern history and values. To have taken up arms against the South was tantamount to declaring war on family. This Lee would not—could not—do. All of his skill, training, knowledge, and determination were now at the service of the newly declared Confederate States of America.

CHAPTER 6

Sidelined

Sometime in the mid-morning, April 23, 1861, Robert E. Lee did something he managed to avoid for much of his life: He delivered a public speech. He had just reported to work on his first day commanding Virginia's armed forces when four gentlemen whisked him to the capital, where the State Convention was in full session. After a short delay cooling his heels while motions on the floor were concluded, Lee was led to the speaker's rostrum. The Convention's president, John Janney, smoothly reeled off a five-minute speech announcing the fact of Lee's appointment and praising his exemplary service record. Then it was Lee's turn. He likely had anticipated that this might happen, so his characteristically brief acceptance speech was more than improvised and a little less than planned.

Mr. President and Gentlemen of the Convention.
Profoundly impressed with the solemnity of the occasion, for which
I must say I was not prepared, I accept the position assigned me by
your partiality. I would have much preferred had your choice fallen
on an abler man. Trusting in Almighty God, an approving con-
science, and the aid of my fellow-citizens, I devote myself to the
service of my native State, in whose behalf alone will I ever again
draw my sword.[1]

It was pure Lee. Square on topic and gently self-deprecating,
he relied on God while promising to do his all. Once freed from
the public ceremonies, Lee turned his attention to meeting Virginia's military needs. Troops were mobilized, drilled, and dispatched to strategic points around the state. Needing drillmasters,
he turned to the Virginia Military Institute and deployed fuzz-
cheeked cadets to supplement his thin cadres of experienced officers teaching older volunteers the rudiments of military
evolutions. Working mostly out of Richmond, Lee pieced together
a credible defensive web.

In the midst of this nonstop activity, he learned that his wife
had been forced to move out of her beloved Arlington mansion,
which was promptly taken over by Federal authorities. Although
Mary protested mightily, the deed was done and there was nothing
that Robert Edward could do to ameliorate the situation. "Our private distresses, we must bear with resignation like Christians & not
aggravate them by repining," he lectured her via post.[2]

Lee was a professional realist tossed about in a sea of amateur
war enthusiasts who were convinced that the fighting would be
short and conclusive, and the sooner it started the better. Much
against his recommendation that soldiers be kept in ranks for the
duration of the emergency, the Convention voted to make all Virginia enlistments twelve-month terms. "The war may last ten
years," was Lee's gloomy assessment to his wife.[3]

Nothing remained the same for very long. On April 24, Virginia (still a sovereign body politic) entered into a military alliance with the Confederate States and Lee was tasked with mustering state units into the ranks of the Confederate army, a process he finished by June 8. He increasingly was caught between two civil powers: Virginia and the Confederate States of America, which was gradually assuming military authority over his state. Lee courteously declined an initial offer to join the Confederacy at its highest authorized rank, that of brigadier general. It was an offer that Lee's ambitious friend and fellow West Pointer Joseph E. Johnston would not refuse.

Soon Lee had a different chain of command. As the new government moved lock, stock, and barrel from Montgomery, Alabama, to Richmond, the existing Virginia military structures were folded into Confederate ones. This time Lee accepted his reranking as a brigadier general in the CSA. With the Dominion State shaping up to be the war's first major theater of operations, CSA President Jefferson Davis began to have regular meetings with the man who had laid the groundwork for its defense. Lee was kept in the planning office as critical eastern field appointments went to officers longer connected to the Confederacy or held in higher regard by Davis—Joseph E. Johnston and P. G. T. Beauregard.

Lee was in something of an administrative no-man's-land, free to act with authority in certain areas, while subordinate in others. Among the distant officers that Lee began to know and appreciate at this time was the quirky yet aggressively competent Virginia Military Institute instructor Thomas J. Jackson, who held the exposed post at Harper's Ferry until Johnston superseded him. Lee and Johnston soon found themselves at opposite ends of a policy argument. Lee (along with Jackson) thought it worth the risk to keep the Harper's Ferry arsenal operating as long as possible, while Johnston wanted to abandon the outpost soonest. For the moment Lee's counsel held sway, but Johnston's gaze was constantly over his shoulder where all sorts of enemy threats apparently loomed. Johnston abandoned Harper's Ferry in mid-June with no warning to President Davis or Lee and many scarce supplies were destroyed during the hasty departure.

The South's other leading general, P. G. T. Beauregard, was also proving to be a thorn in Davis's side. Watching over the important railroad hub at Manassas Junction, Beauregard submitted plan after plan for risky maneuvers promising high returns. There was quibbling galore as Beauregard and Johnston pushed back against Davis's tendency to interfere with what they saw as their prerogatives, while the President was adamant that the military regulations laid down by the Confederate Congress be obeyed to the letter. Lee did his best to steer clear of the squabbles.

Richmond erupted in commotion and excitement on July 21, when word came of the war's opening clash near Manassas Junction. With hardly a by-your-leave to his military advisor, President Davis commandeered a locomotive and rushed to the scene. Robert E. Lee could only wait with the rest of the city as bits and pieces of the story clattered down the telegraph wire. Not until after dark did Davis send the definitive word: "We have won a glorious though dear-bought victory."[4] Often overlooked in analyzing the Rebel success was the use of rail transportation to bring Johnston's force to the battlefield in time to make a difference, a suggestion that originated with Lee. Writing soon afterward to his wife about missing the start of the shooting war, Lee complained: "I wished to partake in the . . . struggle, and am mortified at my absence."[5]

For the first but not last time in the widening conflict, a battlefield victory proved anything but decisive. When Beauregard persisted in trying to have his way despite regulations, and attempted to put political pressures on Davis to get what he wanted, the CSA president reassigned the Confederacy's first hero to a western post in January 1862, about as far from Richmond as was possible, leaving central Virginia's military forces in Johnston's hands.

Lee was finally dispatched to an active theater. He was not directed to any of the critical areas, though, but instead was sent to northwestern Virginia and thrust into a situation that would soon have him at wits' end. That mountainous portion of the state, perhaps the most pro-Union region of any, had been quiet until mid-July when a Federal column invaded from the west and scattered the first defenders it encountered.

Lee's mission was to both report on the situation and advise the three officers responsible for holding the region. The advice part might have worked if those men were joined in a common cause, but as Lee soon discovered, discord was their dominate theme. Two of the officers were former Virginia governors who heartily disliked and distrusted each other. The third was equally determined to operate independent of outsiders. Distant Richmond and Lee were viewed with much suspicion.

Lee was much appalled by what he saw upon his arrival. The troops were poorly outfitted and even more poorly disciplined. Their camps were breeding grounds for disease; indeed, as he complained, "those on sick list would [themselves] form an army."[6] As he cajoled and importuned the mismatched trio into acting in concert, Lee demonstrated a reasoned commitment to the offensive. His long-term goal was to defeat the enemy, but to get there he accepted the necessity of first improving overall security. To armchair strategists tucked in newspaper offices, Lee seemed to lack sufficient martial spirit. "I am sorry . . . ," he wrote to Mary at one particularly trying point, "that the movements of the armies cannot keep pace with the expectations of the editors of papers."[7]

In much the same way that Winfield Scott had overcome deteriorating conditions after his capture of Veracruz, Lee kept his eyes on the prize so that by mid-September he had garnered sufficient cooperation to attack an exposed Federal post on Cheat Mountain. He concocted a converging surprise assault on the enemy camp involving several columns; the fighting was to begin when one specific colonel reached a key position and opened fire. On the day of the action, September 12, Lee waited in vain for the sound of musketry. It turned out that the colonel in question, duped by a tall tale spun by a Union POW that the camp was fully alert and heavily reinforced, decided on his own to cancel the operation. For Lee, his frustrations concerning officers who would not follow orders was tempered with sorrow over the loss of a close associate in the action and pride at the fine scouting work carried out by cavalry units commanded by his son Fitzhugh ("Rooney").

Back in Richmond, the Confederacy had at long last authorized the rank of full general and on August 31 President Davis announced the first four to be promoted. Lee came in third, behind Samuel Cooper and Albert Sidney Johnston, and ahead of Joseph E. Johnston. (Before his break with Davis, P. G. T. Beauregard would be added as number five for his Manassas Junction achievements.) For the rank-conscious Joe Johnston, coming after Lee on the seniority list was a professional slight that would forever rankle.

Lee's struggles in the region that in a year-and-a-half would join the United States as West Virginia ended in late October when he was recalled to Richmond for a new posting. On the plus side, he returned with more field experience under his belt and the knowledge that to command was to command. Moving forward, he was determined to acquire sufficient authority to act, and to use that authority to its fullest. He also departed with the happy memory of riding a young horse whose strength and endurance had met his every need. The animal's name was Greenbrier and Lee would come to know him again.

Lee enjoyed a week in Richmond with his family before continuing southward to take charge of a recently constituted military department covering the coastal regions of South Carolina, Georgia, and eastern Florida. He set up shop in a dumpy village on the Savannah and Charleston Railroad known as Coosawhatchie.

While to the public view he maintained a professional demeanor and attitude, his private frustrations were close to the boiling point. "Another forlorn hope expedition," he griped to daughter Mildred. "Worse than western Virginia."[8] In a pattern only too common throughout the South, Lee discovered local defensive priorities were informed by political needs and propertied interests over legitimate military considerations.

This time Lee was acting with more direct authority than he had previously enjoyed, though he was sage enough to recognize that winning hearts and minds mattered as much as issuing directives. With the U.S. Navy dominating most coastal waterways, he had to draw the defensive line along interior points where land batteries stood a chance against naval broadsides. Lee's policies made him few friends among the rich and powerful whose extensive coastal plantations were left exposed, but the Virginian saw no way around it. Fortunately, the Federals showed little initiative at this stage. "I hope the enemy will be polite enough to wait for us," he wrote to his daughters toward the end of the year.[9]

In another pattern reminiscent of his U.S. Army service, the job in hand was far from complete when Lee was recalled to Richmond. With him on his return was a permanent addition to his entourage, the gray stallion he had so admired in western Virginia. The horse and its owner had providentially been transferred to South Carolina, where Lee quickly closed the deal. Greenbrier was soon renamed Traveler.

Back in the Confederate capital, there were rumors that Lee would be secretary of war, but it was just talk. In another action, Congress attempted to create a new position overseeing all Rebel armies, but Jefferson Davis vetoed it. (He had actually proposed the legislative measure but withdrew his support when Congress broadened the independent authority the officer would enjoy.) Lee returned to the status of military advisor to the president, not an easy task when the person in question regarded himself as a superior military thinker. As was his wont, Lee kept his real feelings all in the family. "I do not see either advantage or pleasure in my duties," he confided to Mary.[10]

Shortly before Lee resumed station in Richmond, another crisis rippled through Richmond courtesy of Joe Johnston, holding the Rebel line near Manassas. Just as at Harper's Ferry, Johnston became increasingly anxious about enemy schemes to cut him off, coupled with a belief that his situation was not being taken seriously in Richmond. Convinced that the Federals were about to act, Johnston precipitately pulled back to the line of the Rappahannock River, so quickly that 1.5 million pounds of supplies had to be destroyed. Despite having previously approved such a movement in principle, President Davis began to wonder about Johnston's fighting spirit.

One problem area Lee was able to address was that of military manpower. The short-term volunteer system worked well enough in the first flush of war enthusiasm but as it became more and more obvious to everyone that the conflict would be a long one, provisions needed to be made to maintain a sufficient number of men in the ranks. With Davis's firm approval, Lee had his aide Charles Marshall (a peacetime lawyer) draft a conscription bill for the Confederate Congress. The elected officials poked and prodded the draft, and added a raft of exemptions that Lee thought unwise, before passing it on April 16, 1862, well before any similar action in the North.

Increasingly, all eyes were turning to the eastern tip of Virginia's Peninsula, near Fort Monroe, where a huge U.S. army was assembling after being transported from the Washington area. At the height of the Revolutionary War, George Washington was lucky to have more than 20,000 men under his direct command at any one time. Now the Union force under Major General George B. McClellan was topping 100,000. Arrayed against it were just a few thousand Rebel soldiers led by Major General John B. Magruder.

Responding to this threat again cast Joe Johnston and Lee on opposite sides.

At about 10:00 A.M., April 14, President Davis convened an urgent council of war. Present in addition to Lee and Johnston were the new secretary of war, George W. Randolph, and Johnston's two senior subcommanders, generals Gustavus W. Smith and James Longstreet. Johnston had initially welcomed orders transferring some of his units from the quiet Rappahannock front to the Peninsula, but now wanted to meet the enemy buildup by concentrating all available troops near Richmond, gambling everything on one titanic battle. Toward that end he was prepared to yield the entire Peninsula without a fight. Lee, anxious to contest every inch of any enemy advance, urged that Magruder be further reinforced.

Secretary of War Randolph backed Lee with another argument. Pulling back from the eastern Peninsula would uncover the port of Norfolk, site of the all-important Gosport Navy Yard and home base for the Confederacy's first and most successful wonder weapon, the ironclad C.S.S. *Virginia* (aka the *Merrimac*). The armored vessel, which had savaged wooden Federal blockaders in Hampton Roads on March 8 only to be met and battled to a draw the next day by the just-arrived Federal ironclad U.S.S. *Monitor,* had no place to go. It drew too much water to run upriver, and was never meant to operate in the open ocean. As long as it was present, even at anchor, it seriously restricted Union naval operations along the James River. Norfolk's fall would doom the vessel.

At the weary end of the seemingly endless discussion, Davis supported the Lee-Randolph position by instructing Johnston to send more troops to Magruder. While Lee returned to handling urgent calls for help from the distant corners of the Confederacy, Johnston followed orders, albeit very slowly and with great caution. His fretting increased as McClellan methodically prepared to challenge Magruder's entrenched lines with overwhelming man- and firepower. Finally, on the night of May 3, Johnston, convinced an attack was imminent, began a general pull-back toward Richmond. As feared and predicted, when Norfolk could not be held the *Virginia* was immolated by its crew on May 11.

Joseph E. Johnston demonstrated a "how-not-to" in civilian-military relationships by consistently undertaking significant strategic movements without informing either President Davis or advisor Lee of his actions. At the same time Lee was quietly working the edges of his authority to meet a new threat to Richmond. His actions in the weeks to come revealed another aspect of his military acumen, an ability to see connections between seemingly distant and separate theaters of operations.

A Union force of 30,000 plus had marched from near Washington to Fredericksburg, Virginia, where it was poised to continue south for a linkup with McClellan to march up the Peninsula. The way responsibilities were parceled out, it was Joe Johnston's task to respond, but he showed scant interest in the sector. Lee happily moved into the power vacuum.

He guessed that the enemy force would have to increase before it could tackle Richmond. The most likely source for those reinforcements were Yankee units already deployed in the Shenandoah Valley. If those distant troops could be prevented from reaching Fredericksburg, the entire enterprise might die aborning.

Lee found a kindred spirit in the Southern general commanding in the Valley, Major General Thomas J. Jackson who, ever since his performance during the Manassas battle, had been nicknamed "Stonewall." Quietly and without consulting Johnston, Lee began to reinforce Jackson and counsel him on tackling the enemy's troops in the valley. It was a challenging tightrope to walk. Lee had no authority to order Jackson to take action and could only endorse and encourage any decision he made to fight. Johnston could interpose himself at any time, and indeed, he did issue instructions that would have ended one offensive gambit had not Jackson (seconded by Lee) found a way to circumvent his orders.

Johnston's own considerable anxieties and distractions provided one reason why Lee was able to pursue his scheme without much interference. Another was the growing confidence placed in him by Jefferson Davis. A final reason was Jackson's wholehearted support and fierce determination to undertake the mission.

While Lee was surreptitiously pulling these strings, Richmond lurched to a panic point. Just one day after the *Virginia* was destroyed, a flotilla of U.S. warships that included the *Monitor* began ascending the James River, intent on bombarding Richmond. All that stood in the way was a hastily constructed defensive position on Drewry's Bluff called Fort Darling, augmented by some obstructions placed below it in the river.

Lee was summoned to a quickly assembled Cabinet meeting where he found plans being urgently discussed to abandon the capital. When his turn came, Lee's response to the crisis was simple and forceful. "Richmond must not be given up," he insisted, "it shall not be given up!"[11] The evacuation decision was still on hold as the meeting ended. The next day, May 15, the U.S. ships blasted at Fort Darling but were unable to silence it. Once it became clear that the vessels were taking more damage than they were inflicting, the Yankee sailors withdrew and Richmond breathed a sigh of relief.

A week earlier, Lee and Jackson's careful planning had begun to bear fruit. On May 8 at McDowell, Stonewall engaged and defeated an isolated segment of the enemy's larger force. This inaugurated a grueling campaign of hard marching in unexpected directions to strike where least anticipated. Fighting occurred at Front Royal on May 23, outside Winchester on May 25, at Cross Keys on June 8, and Port Republic on June 9. Each time Jackson did the attacking and the Federals did the withdrawing. By the campaign's end, the Union force at Fredericksburg was frozen in place while Jackson enjoyed complete freedom of movement. Lee's strategic framework and Jackson's inspired execution had eliminated the northern threat to Richmond. The only problem left was McClellan's massive army, now within sight of the city's tallest church spires.

True to his original (rejected) plan, Joe Johnston had fallen back to Richmond's outskirts. Time and again, Lee had watched with concern as Johnston bypassed several naturally strong defensive points without attempting any delaying effort. First Davis, and then Lee, pressed Johnston to make a stand. Finally, with his back literally to the wall, Johnston at last saw an opportunity to overwhelm a portion of McClellan's army isolated on the south side of the Chickahominy River. Those two Union corps became the focus of a complicated converging attack employing four Confederate divisions to assail them from three directions.

On the day of battle, May 31, just about nothing went as Johnston intended. In the end, only portions of two divisions got into action, while the Federals received timely reinforcements. Some 6,000 Rebel soldiers fell, while 5,000 Yankees were killed, wounded, or captured with no major change in their positions. Johnston himself, observing the Confederate fighting from a knoll 200 yards north of Fair Oaks Station, was counted among the Southern casualties. He was hit twice, once by a bullet in the right shoulder followed almost immediately by a piece of artillery shell that punched him off his horse. Command devolved to Gustavus Smith, who had limited knowledge of Johnston's plan and even less nerve to manage in a crisis. When Jefferson Davis met with Smith that night he came away certain that a change had to be made if disaster was to be avoided.

There was nothing exceptional about Davis's quick determination to hand over the army to Robert E. Lee. Rank, experience, and seniority all supported the decision. If Davis did have any regrets, they were likely in the nature of losing a utility man of Lee's abilities and not being able to take charge himself. The brief message officially notifying Lee of the command change was dutifully transmitted early on June 1.

Everything about Lee's actions from this day forward indicates that he was a man who was primed for the challenge. His objective was clear: Save Richmond. His unspoken purpose was equally clear: Destroy the enemy's will to prosecute this war. Lee was prepared to accept great risks to succeed, and to utilize every resource he could summon to the fight. Nothing would be held back. From this day forward, the Civil War in Virginia changed.

CHAPTER 7

The Seven Days

Robert E. Lee's primary objective upon taking command was expressed in a comment made to his military secretary, A. L. Long, as the two surveyed the distant Union lines on June 16. "Now, Colonel Long," Lee asked, "how can we get at those people?"[1] Another insight into his thinking came at his first meeting with his principal subcommanders two weeks earlier. After listening attentively as one officer dourly itemized the enemy's advantages in manpower and weaponry, Lee cut him off. "Stop, stop," he said, "if you go to ciphering we are whipped beforehand."[2]

Lee was thinking offensively, but as he had done in western Virginia, he first made sure that Richmond's defenses could withstand a hard blow. Orders were issued detailing picks and shovels to the soldiers and directing them to improve the capital's earthworks.

For the moment Lee was seen as anything but a fighting general, the most popular sobriquet being "King of Spades."[3]

However, going after McClellan was very much on his mind. For a brief period he gave serious consideration to a strategic proposal from Stonewall Jackson in the Shenandoah Valley. Were Lee to increase the Valley Army to 40,000 men, Jackson was prepared to march into Pennsylvania, an action that would surely cause Mc-Clellan to detach help. Upon more considered reflection, Lee passed Jackson's request along to Jefferson Davis with the comment that any significant reinforcement would have to come from Rebel forces in Georgia, South Carolina, and North Carolina. As this was patently impossible, Jackson's scheme was quietly shelved, but not forgotten (though Lee did send Jackson reinforcements roughly equal to his battle losses).

Throughout what Lee had officially designated the Army of Northern Virginia, men and officers tried to take a measure of their new commander. Among those with questions was a promising artilleryman, E. P. Alexander. Roughly two weeks after Lee had taken charge, Alexander found himself with an officer he respected from President Davis's staff and asked him point blank if he thought Lee had audacity sufficient for the job. "Alexander," the confidant replied, "if there is one man in either army, Federal or Confederate, who is, head & shoulders, far above every other one in either army in audacity that man is Gen. Lee, and you will very soon have lived to see it. Lee is audacity personified."[4]

Before he could demonstrate this audacity, Lee had a personal matter requiring felicity. His wife, intent on watching over her son Rooney's White House property inherited from her father, had been slow to evacuate and was stuck behind enemy lines for a second time. Union general McClellan graciously allowed Lee to send an escort for his wife so she could relocate to Richmond, which he did on June 10. The evidence is that Lee was too busy planning his upcoming offensive to spend more than a few moments with her when she reached him at Meadow Bridge. The business of war was all-consuming.

What Lee needed most of all was a clear picture of the enemy's position. On June 10 he met with his cavalry chief, Brigadier General "Jeb" Stuart, to request a reconnaissance of McClellan's right flank, which Lee sensed was vulnerable. Stuart did his chief one better, proposing he make a complete circuit of the enemy. Not only would it allow him to fully scout McClellan's right wing, Stuart argued, but it would effectively mask the operation's true purpose. While not on record as formally approving the proposed action, Lee did not say no, so early on the morning of June 12 Stuart and 1,200 picked horsemen (including Rooney Lee's regiment) departed Richmond following a roundabout route to the enemy's rear.

Three days later, even as the Southern press found something to ballyhoo in Stuart's daring deed, the cavalryman was briefing Lee. A single Union corps was practically isolated on the north side of the Chickahominy River, with its advance outposts in the village of Mechanicsville. Its right flank was wide open to a force approaching from the northeast. Lee wasted no time. On June 16, Stonewall Jackson received his orders to bring the Valley Army to Richmond. "The sooner you unite with this army the better," said Lee.[5]

Throughout these busy days, Lee maintained regular contact with Jefferson Davis. He kept him informed of conditions at the front, shared some of his thinking, and even solicited opinions regarding certain matters. The fact that the enemy stood at Richmond's very gates allowed the two to work in smooth tandem, masking a deep divide between them regarding grand strategy.

Davis believed that the South would win this war through an essentially defensive posture. By boldly protecting its territorial boundaries, the Confederacy would outlast the North's waning will to continue the contest and survive long enough to garner recognition from the international community. Lee felt that the South's survival demanded a decisive defeat of the enemy's field armies. Turning back any invaders merely granted the South breathing space and time, something that the technologically superior and more heavily populated North would eventually use to win. Wrecking enemy armies would force the North to the peace table well before its advantages could be felt.

Now armed with the solid intelligence provided by Stuart's ride, Lee summoned his top commanders to him on the afternoon of June 23. Present in addition to Lee were Stonewall Jackson (who had just arrived after a grueling fifty-plus mile ride), Daniel Harvey Hill ("D. H."), Ambrose Powell Hill ("A. P.," no relation), and James Longstreet. Lee quickly established his mission goals: to crush the enemy's right flank and then to roll up as much of it as possible once it was flushed from its entrenchments and forced to protect its supply line running east to White House, on the Pamunkey River. The two Hills and Longstreet would press the front, while Jackson would come in on roads leading into the enemy's rear area. A huddle among the officers came up with June 26 as the earliest feasible date to commence the action. Lee sent them back to their commands and wrote out his battle orders on June 24.

On June 25 the Rebel units committed to the attack moved into jump-off positions. In order to achieve the necessary concentration of forces, Lee cut the number of men holding Richmond's southern defensive lines to a bare minimum, leaving some 28,900 soldiers facing 76,000. For a few nerve-wracking hours it seemed that McClellan was calling Lee's bluff when fighting erupted that morning in front of those very lines. "I fear from the operations of the enemy . . . that our plan of operation has been discovered to them," Lee worried to Davis at the height of the combat. Not until the afternoon did it become evident that the scuffle was a probe aimed more at straightening out twisted picket lines than forcing the main entrenchments. Writing that evening to President Davis, Lee said: "I have determined to make no change in the plan."[6]

Lee expected the battle to begin between 8 and 9:00 A.M. on June 26. He had done his best to assure himself of local superiority of numbers. Altogether his plan concentrated some 55,800 men against a Union force roughly half that size. Even with these advantages, Lee worried about his outnumbered defenders holding Richmond's entrenched lines. Orders sent late that day to the officer in charge there exhorted him to maintain his position "at the point of the bayonet if necessary."[7]

Morning passed with nothing more than random picket firing along the lines. Lee knew from an early message that Jackson was running late, but having the Valley Army in position behind the enemy flank was critical to the plan, so he waited. Once Jackson was ready, A. P. Hill was cued to attack from off Jackson's right flank. Not helping matters was the presence of President Davis, who had arrived at the front at about 2:00 P.M. in the company of Secretary of War Randolph and Secretary of the Navy Stephen R. Mallory.

Finally, at about 4:00 P.M., the spotty musketry crescendoed. Looking through his glasses, Lee could see Yankee pickets tumbling back to their main line, closely pursued by a heavy skirmish line. "Those are Hill's men," Lee announced with some relief, before turning to James Longstreet. "General," he said, "you may now cross over." The battle was joined.[8]

It took a short, sharp combat to push the Federals out of Mechanicsville. Once it was clear that the fighting front had migrated east, Lee entered the captured village to confer with A. P. Hill. Here he learned that Hill actually had no idea whether or not Jackson's men were in position. Not hearing from Stonewall and fearing that doing nothing was the worst option, Hill decided to launch a limited advance to capture Mechanicsville in order to clear the way for follow-up units. Hill's action committed Lee to up the ante. He had

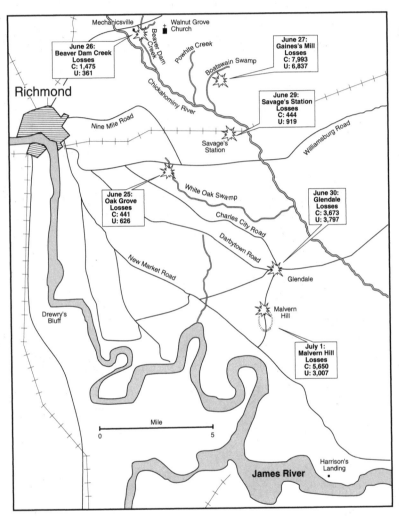

Mechanicsville
Walnut Grove Church

June 26:
Beaver Dam Creek
Losses
C: 1,475
U: 361

Beaver Dam Creek

Powhite Creek

Chickahominy River

Boatswain Swamp

June 27:
Gaines's Mill
Losses
C: 7,993
U: 6,837

Richmond

Nine Mile Road

June 29:
Savage's Station
Losses
C: 444
U: 919

Williamsburg Road

Savage's Station

White Oak Swamp

June 25:
Oak Grove
Losses
C: 441
U: 626

Charles City Road

June 30:
Glendale
Losses
C: 3,673
U: 3,797

Darbytown Road

New Market Road

Glendale

Drewry's Bluff

Malvern Hill

July 1:
Malvern Hill
Losses
C: 5,650
U: 3,007

Mile

0   5

Harrison's Landing

James River

THE SEVEN DAYS

to assume that the Federals would realize he had massed his forces north of the Chickahominy River at the risk of his lines below that point. To keep McClellan's attention on him and not his undermanned defenses, Lee had to turn Hill's limited advance into a larger attack.

More men from A. P. Hill's division were committed, along with several brigades from D. H. Hill's command. Even as Lee was working to choreograph this dramatic change of plans, Jefferson Davis and his entourage reached Mechanicsville. Observing the party arrive, Lee rode over and asked: "Mr. President, am I in command here?" When Davis agreed, Lee continued: "Then I forbid you to stand here under the enemy's guns. Any exposure of a life like yours is wrong. And this is useless exposure. You must go back."[9] Reluctantly acceding to Lee's request, Davis led his party toward the rear, retiring only until they were out of Lee's sight when they resumed their observation.

Lee was learning that it was one thing to initiate a battle, quite another to control it. Troops would be called forward to exploit what seemed to be a breakthrough or called up to rescue other units pinned down only to find themselves attacking alone in the face of terrific fire. The Yankees had fallen back to a naturally strong line behind Beaver Dam Creek, a swampy stream with briery banks that funneled attackers into perfect targets. Charge after charge just ran out of steam as soldiers struggled against obstacles natural and manmade. Not until dark did the shooting finally stop.

Lee's confident battle plan had proven no more viable than Johnston's at Seven Pines. Thanks to a litany of miscues and confusion over changes in orders, barely one-fifth of the Rebel troops on hand were engaged. Lee's failures this day included poor staff work, nonexistent monitoring of Jackson's critical movements, and misinformation from subordinates regarding changing circumstances. Tactically, Lee's first battle commanding the Army of Northern Virginia, was a defeat.

There is no evidence that he spent much time this night in self-recriminations. The enemy was still there and he remained determined to strike a blow that would shatter McClellan's army. In the pre-dawn of June 27, Confederate pickets reported that the enemy was withdrawing. Not needing any orders from above, local commanders organized advances and by the time the sun rose above the horizon, Union positions that had been held against assault on June 26 were now Rebel-occupied with hardly a struggle. Lee felt that he could not let up the pressure for even a moment. The enemy on this flank was out of its trenches and on the move, perhaps heavily damaged from yesterday's fighting. Allowing the Federals time to regroup and rethink would squander the precious initiative his men now possessed.

Looking at his map, Lee anticipated the enemy making a stand behind Powhite Creek, perhaps four miles to the southeast. Orders sent various divisions onto roads converging at the watercourse from the northwest, while Jackson's men (all of whom missed the June 26 fight) were again targeted against the enemy's rear.

Learning that Jackson was present at Walnut Grove Church, Lee rode there to meet with him in person. Neither left a record of their conversation, nor was anyone else close enough to overhear. Most likely, Jackson was briefed on his route and the importance of his movement. Chastisement was not Lee's style, so it's unlikely Jackson was taken to task for his poor performance on June 26. Lee also lacked enough training to recognize the near total state of exhaustion that had so dulled (and would continue to befog) the instincts of one of the South's premier fighters.

It was no simple task to move one army in pursuit of another, and the disparate elements under Lee's direction were an army in name only. The hot, sultry morning passed without combat as officers and columns tramped along barely defined roadways in the stifling atmosphere using maps filled with more guesswork than certainty. One significant advantage was gained when Lee's men found New Bridge across the Chickahominy merely damaged by the retreating Federals and quickly repairable. Lee would now be in easy communication with his thinned Richmond lines just in case the enemy turned that way. Another plus was the link-up between Lee's and Jackson's armies around midday, though it was preceded by a brief exchange of friendly fire that fortunately did no damage.

Success in battle rarely sits only on one side, and Lee's positive run was about to end. A brigade of South Carolinians that he was accompanying arrived at Powhite Creek to find it held by a skeleton force that was easily dispersed. However, the Rebel soldiers then advanced only a short distance beyond the stream before they were staggered by a shower of shells and bullets. A member of Marmaduke Johnson's Jackson Artillery anxiously watched as Lee and his aides passed through random fire that nicked horses and men in his battery. Then a body of South Carolina troops came streaming back in a panic. Rounding up some of the mounted soldiers around him, Lee said: "Gentlemen, we must rally those men."[10]

Even as this local crisis was brought under control, there were other unsettling signs that everything was not as Lee's lieutenants had imagined them to be. Jackson's leading division, coming down from the north, butted up against a strongly held enemy line where there wasn't supposed to be one. The Federals were well posted behind a swampy creek not on any map, and, even more disconcerting, Jackson's men were facing them head-on instead of striking their underside. Word of this encounter percolated up the chain of command to Jackson, who failed to immediately inform Lee of the new circumstances.

Even without an update from Jackson, Lee was forced to revise his mental map of the position taken by McClellan's army as reports arrived from other officers. The enemy was present in strength, stoutly positioned behind a stream and brushy swamp not on any Confederate map. A local man was finally located who identified it as Boatswain's Swamp. Still intent on striking the Federals this day, Lee began directing his arriving units into positions along the Union perimeter. At no point did he consider not attacking with every rifle available to him, some 54,300 by rough count. Everyone was in place by 2:30 P.M., when the South Carolinians resumed the contest.

The first phase of what would be known as the Battle of Gaines's Mill unfolded as a series of hard strikes against the Union line, which lashed back with deadly torrents of artillery and musketry. Individual courage was in generous supply and sacrificial heroism common. Losses among the most valiant leaders were especially steep. The Union line was well knitted together and stolidly held. After more than an hour of seeing the separate assaults stopped in a bloody welter, Lee realized that nothing less than a single combined effort could hope to succeed.

Lee visited Jackson, who had yet to commit his full weight to the combat. Some of his disappointment with Jackson's performance thus far seeped into his greeting. "Ah, General," said Lee, "I am very glad to see you. I had hoped to be with you before." Jackson merely nodded in return. Continued Lee: "That fire is very heavy. Do you think your men can stand it?" This roused the taciturn officer to a response: "They can stand almost anything. They can stand that!"[11]

The concerted effort Lee finally organized was hardly out of Currier and Ives, but most of the units got the idea and plowed into the fray. The breakthrough Lee had been seeking all afternoon came courtesy of Brigadier General William H. C. Whiting's division, whose Texas and Georgia troops simply would not be denied. The Federal position began to collapse in the dimming twilight, some units pulling back in good order, others dissolving in exhausted panic.

There were 22 Yankee cannon captured and 2,829 prisoners taken. In his brief dispatch to Jefferson Davis announcing the results, Lee thanked God for the "signal victory" and acknowledged that the "loss in officers and men is great." Lee's closing words to Davis made it clear that he was far from finished. "We sleep on the field, and shall renew the contest in the morning," he said.[12]

On the morning of June 28, Robert E. Lee set out on missions personal and professional. He attended to the personal when he located the Rockbridge Artillery attached to Jackson's command, where he found his son, cannoneer Robert Jr., asleep under a caisson, weary but unhurt. The professional items took more time.

The Confederate victory at Gaines's Mill had knocked the enemy back across the Chickahominy River, itself an effective barrier. McClellan still held his strong earthworks fronting Richmond to the south, making it difficult to ascertain exactly what he was doing. In his advance up the Peninsula, McClellan had established a supply depot on the Pamunkey River at White House, which lay off to the east. If he was planning to retrace his steps, McClellan would have to keep the White House depot in operation; if not, he would abandon it. To find out, a mixed cavalry/infantry force led by Jeb Stuart moved out to investigate.

Throughout the early hours, Lee's men undertook the doleful task of policing the battlefield. Bodies were buried, the wounded collected for transport to Richmond, and equipment of all kinds gathered in. A Georgia soldier was certain that if the women of the North and South could view the carnage, "there would be a ten fold greater clamor for peace among them than there ever was for war."[13]

Late in the day word came from the ever-reliable Stuart that McClellan had burned a critical railroad bridge, severing his supply line, and strongly implying he had finished using the Pamunkey depot. (Lee would find out afterward that the White House mansion itself, part of his son Rooney's inheritance from his grandfather, had been burned in the process.) Stuart's news suggested that McClellan was moving south, toward the James River. By the time he could verify Stuart's information, darkness put an end to operations. Lee worked through the night plotting multiple intercept courses involving his entire army—including units that had been holding the exposed southern front at the time of Gaines's Mill. No longer was he attempting to draw McClellan out of his earthworks. Now the game was a stern chase. The Yankees would have to bunch up while passing through White Oak Swamp, where Lee hoped to catch them.

However, the great battle Lee had been seeking on June 29 did not happen. While he had counted on the enemy columns becoming snarled as they threaded through White Oak Swamp, he had not reckoned that his own troops would suffer in a similar fashion. Only one division actually engaged the Federals in a late afternoon scrap at Savage's Station.

Even though nothing was gained on the Confederate side, this action did mark the debut of an experimental weapon of Lee's design—a 32-pounder cannon mounted on a railroad flatcar, protected in front by a sloping metal plate. It was only in action for a short while before it was driven off by flanking parties of U.S. snipers. Trying to coordinate the movements of so many columns clearly overtaxed Lee and his staff; as a result Stonewall Jackson had to choose between conflicting assignments and was unable to provide battlefield support when it was requested. In a message he sent that day to one of his lieutenants, Lee gave voice to the concern that was steadily obsessing him: "We must lose no more time or he will escape us entirely."[14]

Lee's management style up to now had been "hands-off." Orders were issued and subordinates were expected to execute them. Given the poor results, he changed his style; on June 30 he would be very much "hands-on." Lee was in motion at 3:30 A.M. and in the course of the day met with each of his principal subcommanders, some more than once. The enemy's course converged at Glendale, where he was determined to bring all his available force to bear in order to slice McClellan's army in twain.

The battle that crowned this day at Glendale, known locally as Frayser's Farm, proved anything but climactic. Lee was no more immune from the fog of battle than his lieutenants. His misreading of several visual and aural cues, compounded by entire columns becoming lost or stalled by blocked roads while others engaged in time-consuming countermarches, resulted in just a fraction of his force engaging the enemy. The fight was brutal and hand to hand at times, but in the end the Federal defenses held. Once again President Davis led a small column of onlookers into a hot zone, even with Lee present. This time it took a stern warning from the local commander, A. P. Hill, to move everyone back to a safe distance.

Months into the future, when time allowed Lee to be dispassionate, he would look back at the opportunities lost on June 30 and observe: "Could the other commands have co-operated in the action the result would have proved most disastrous to the enemy."[15] Lee's postmortem has been seconded by historians of the campaign, who agree that Glendale offered him his best opportunity to deliver a shattering blow to McClellan's army.

In the immediate aftermath, however, Lee was thinking only of the next day. His orders to all units for July 1 were to maintain the pursuit.

During the night the enemy had marched just two miles to take up a new blocking position on Malvern Hill. It was as if nature itself had sculpted an ideal defensive site. Flanking the elevated plateau were deep ravines that frustrated any turning movement. Fronting the hill crest was a relatively open plain, forming a perfect killing ground. Along the hill crest itself, Federal officers had massed their batteries, nearly hub-to-hub in places, strongly supported by infantry. With nature and the artifice of war thus combined, the result was a nearly impregnable position. As a further garnish, the weather was hot and muggy.

It was against this position that Lee now assembled his forces. Once more everyone was bedeviled by the Virginia roads and difficult terrain. There were tie-ups galore as columns took wrong turns or found their passage gridlocked by other units claiming right of way. (Feeling unwell, Lee took a less-active role in managing this day's affairs, though his frustration level was running hot. When a subordinate general worried aloud that the enemy was escaping, Lee was uncharacteristically tart. "Yes," he snapped, "he will get away because I cannot have my orders carried out!"[16]) Not until late in the afternoon were all the players assembled.

No one in command seriously considered trying to take the Yankees head on. "If General McClellan is there in force," D. H. Hill muttered to Lee, "we had better let him alone."[17] There was talk of trying to turn a flank. Longstreet believed enough Confederate cannon could be bunched to blow a hole in the enemy's line. Having no better option, Lee worked off that idea. The plan that emerged, such as it was, called for a massive barrage to wreck the Union defenses. Once openings had been created, it fell to one designated brigade to spearhead a general assault.

Everything that could go wrong, did go wrong. The officer in charge of Lee's reserve artillery apparently never got the word, so a sizable number of Rebel tubes were no-shows. Many that did show were poorly commanded or ineptly managed. Batteries that managed to gallop into action found relatively few open areas available for their use. This meant a piecemeal deployment, making it easy for the far more numerous Yankee guns to blast the Rebel cannoneers as fast as they appeared. Despite this pounding, there were some momentary successes for the Confederate artillery, but not nearly enough to make a difference.

Lee himself added to the confusion. Twice that afternoon he ordered advances based on unverified reports—one of the hasty movement of Federal supply wagons, the other of a Rebel unit supposed to have captured a key jumpoff position. By the time he realized that the softening-up process had failed and that an infantry attack was not warranted, those earlier orders sparked attacks that, in turn, prompted other units to join in. There was little coordination, allowing the Yankees ample time to savage an attacking wave before turning their lethal attention to the next. D. H. Hill, who thought the entire enterprise a bad idea, gave this battle its epitaph when he said: "It was not war, it was murder."[18]

After Malvern Hill there was no combat of any consequence on the Peninsula between the Army of Northern Virginia and the Army of the Potomac. In retrospect, Lee's constant hammering of the Union forces outside Richmond had synchronized almost perfectly with George B. McClellan's decision to withdraw his army (which he believed to be heavily outnumbered). Still, even though their leader may have lost his nerve, the Union soldiers fought hard and well, meeting each thrust with resolution and courage. A high cost had been paid by Lee's army, which had 3,494 killed, 15,758 wounded, and 952 missing for a total of 20,204 lost. Nearly one in four of those who began the campaign had been hit.

The philosophical divide between Jefferson Davis and Lee began to widen from this point. From Davis's perspective, Lee's campaign had succeeded on every level. The enemy threat had been neutralized and Richmond redeemed. While Lee was certainly gratified at no longer having to be yoked to the capital's defense, he was profoundly dissatisfied at his failure to wreck McClellan's command. His final report on the Seven Days made that plain. "Under ordinary circumstances," he wrote, "the Federal army should have been destroyed."[19] A letter to his wife penned in early July gave voice to his underlying motives: "Our enemy has met with a heavy loss from which he must take some time to recover & then recommence his operations."[20]

As long as the enemy had the time and space to recover and recommence operations, Lee knew that the Confederacy's days were numbered.

CHAPTER 8

Raiding North (1)

From the moment he took charge of the Army of Northern Virginia, Lee made it his own. The force he had inherited from Johnston had been slapped together with little thought to the parts connecting the whole. Lee spent time and attention tuning the fighting machine. "Very soon," wrote an officer present, "and almost imperceptibly, the network of the general organization was cast over the whole army, and we were brought into a far closer connection with headquarters."[1]

Soon after the end of the Seven Days campaign, Lee also cleaned house. Top officers whose performances had impressed him were given more responsibility, while those who had seriously disappointed were diplomatically let go. John B. Magruder was allowed to accept a posting west of the Mississippi River, Gustavus W. Smith had his sick leave extended indefinitely, and others were similarly handled. Longstreet and Jackson were each allotted roughly half the army to manage and a number of other deserving lower-grade officers were promoted. Not long after these changes, Jackson declared that such was his confidence in Lee's leadership "that I am willing to follow him blindfolded."[2]

McClellan's curling up into a ball around Harrison's Landing did not end Lee's strategic conundrums. As a force in being, just twenty-three miles from Richmond, it could not be ignored. There was also a footloose Union corps under Ambrose Burnside in transit from North Carolina that could appear at any point. Finally, Washington planners had begun forming a new army in northern Virginia, the core of which consisted of the pieces Jackson had fought in the Shenandoah Valley. To lead them the Lincoln administration imported John Pope, a western general with a record of success. In rhetoric, at least, Pope represented a sea-change from the risk-adverse McClellan. "Success and glory are in the advance," Pope proclaimed, "disaster and shame lurk in the rear."[3]

Pope accompanied his call to arms with draconian measures that especially targeted Virginia civilians. Citizens even suspected of complicity in guerrilla activities could expect little mercy from him. While Pope's policies aroused Lee's ire, the cold fact was that the army taking shape in northern Virginia posed a clear and present danger to Richmond's critical connection to the Shenandoah Valley granaries—the Virginia Central Railroad. The moment Lee learned that Pope's Army of Virginia was concentrating at Culpeper, he knew he had to act.

Stonewall Jackson had already proven himself adept at operating effectively and aggressively in the Valley against a numerically superior enemy, so on July 13 Lee instructed him to take two divisions—some 12,000 men—to suppress Pope. It took six days for Jackson's men to reach the strategically important transportation hub of Gordonsville, just in time to thwart a Union cavalry raid. For the next week or so the two sides confronted each other from a safe distance. Jackson was chafing to go on the offensive, but, as he told Lee, he needed more troops. On July 27 Lee sent a division and a brigade to Jackson, who promptly found an opportunity for attack when Pope's troop movements left a corps exposed. Jackson fought and won a day-long battle at Cedar Mountain on August 9, after which he prudently retreated, since what remained of the Army of Virginia heavily outnumbered him.

Monitoring affairs from outside Richmond, Lee sifted through intelligence reports that made for a disquieting picture. Not only was Burnside's command in motion to reinforce Pope, but portions of McClellan's army were moving in the same direction. Concluding that this was not all some elaborate ruse to expose Richmond to capture, Lee ordered Longstreet with ten brigades to Gordonsville. He identified several other units he wanted with him that were then part of the capital's defense and began jawing with President Davis about releasing them. Lee himself reached Gordonsville on August 15.

In carrying out his own offensive movement, John Pope sandwiched his Army of Virginia between the Rapidan and Rappahannock rivers. Lee proposed to cross the Rapidan to mash Pope against the Rappahannock. His plan called for Jackson's and Longstreet's wings to mass against Pope's left flank while a cavalry brigade under Fitzhugh Lee would swing around Pope's right to choke his escape. Despite the improvements Lee had made to his army's infrastructure, there were critical communication lapses that delayed its consolidation; delays that Pope, suddenly alert to his peril, used to withdraw behind the Rappahannock.

As Pope spread his army to cover the Rappahannock's principal crossing points, time was on his side. Reinforcements were indeed on the way, and the longer he could keep Lee at arm's length, the stronger he became. Lee knew this too and for several days he actively probed the river crossings, hoping to find one Pope had missed. At the same time he obtained permission from Jefferson

Davis to march north of the Rappahannock should circumstances allow. By August 21 Lee had fixed Pope's river line and immediately ordered Jackson's wing with cavalry support to flank it at a point two miles north of where it ended. Once more Pope was able to block the move and once more Lee was stymied.

Stymied but not stopped. Additional patrols sought other crossings and found one at Sulphur Springs, five miles beyond the guarded fords. A new scheme was worked up: Jackson would cross at the Springs while Stuart passed over farther north to take his cavalry on a deep raid into the rear of Pope's army. General Weather unexpectedly intervened with heavy rains that dramatically flooded the river, stranding the one division Jackson had crossed. Stuart managed to complete his raid, which proved more style than substance. After some nerve-wracking days and nights Jackson successfully withdrew his exposed division.

On August 24, it was almost back to square one. Lee's window of opportunity was closing. He either had to back off or take more risks. He chose the latter. On August 25 Jackson's men crossed the Rappahannock at Hinson's Mill Ford, north of Jeffersonton. Jackson's route took him north and then east through Thoroughfare Gap. Ahead of him was a major Federal supply depot at Manassas Junction. Running about a day and a half behind him was Lee, with Longstreet and the rest of the Army of Northern Virginia. If alert Federals could interpose between them, Lee could be beaten in detail; if the halves could be joined then John Pope would find himself with a significant Rebel force separating him from his reinforcements.

In the days following, culminating on August 28–30 with the Battle of Second Manassas, Lee played two roles: He oversaw the military forces soon to be engaged, and he kept a line open to Jefferson Davis, both pressing him for additional reinforcements and making the case to keep going north. For the most part, Davis gave Lee what he wanted in manpower, though the President's

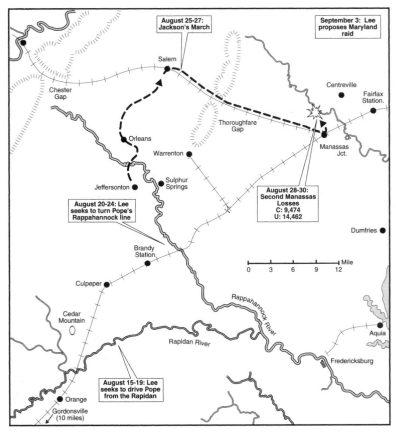

August 25-27: Jackson's March

September 3: Lee proposes Maryland raid

Salem

Chester Gap

Centreville

Fairfax Station.

Thoroughfare Gap

Orleans

Warrenton

Manassas Jct.

August 28-30: Second Manassas Losses
C: 9,474
U: 14,462

Jeffersonton

Sulphur Springs

August 20-24: Lee seeks to turn Pope's Rappahannock line

Dumfries

Brandy Station.

Mile

0   3   6   9   12

Culpeper

Rappahannock River

Cedar Mountain

Aquia

Rapidan River

August 15-19: Lee seeks to drive Pope from the Rapidan

Fredericksburg

Orange

Gordonsville (10 miles)

SUPPRESSING POPE

anxieties regarding Richmond's security were such that he withheld three brigades Lee sought. Lee accepted Davis's decision without histrionics.

In the summaries he provided to the distant Davis, Lee was only partially forthcoming. His intent from the beginning had been to destroy Pope's army; yet, as late as August 30 (after two days of severe combat), Lee told Davis that his "desire has been to avoid a general engagement."[4]

Events suggest otherwise. Following his successful sacking of Manassas Junction (and a feast on Yankee supplies that his soldiers never forgot), Jackson took a position astride Pope's main supply route (while carefully securing a road from Thoroughfare Gap) and picked a fight. He found one on August 28 when he battled a Union division near Groveton. This brought up Pope the next day with the bulk of his army, who vigorously attacked Jackson in the position he held behind an unfinished railroad cut. The fighting was brutally personal at times, but Jackson's men held their ground.

Lee won his gamble at 10:00 A.M. when Longstreet's van approached the battlefield. Eager to size up the engagement, Lee rode forward for a better view of the Yankee lines. When he rejoined his staff, he made the offhand comment, "A Yankee sharpshooter came near killing me just now."[5]

Lee preferred having Longstreet immediately pitch into the fight, but "Old Pete" convinced him that waiting until all the arriving units had been organized into one powerful blow would be better. Everything was in place when the attack got underway about 4:00 P.M., August 30. Incredibly, despite sightings and other evidence of Longstreet's presence, John Pope refused to believe that Lee had reunited his force until it was too late. The Army of Virginia reeled under the hammer blow of Longstreet's attack and began to retreat. This time, however, the Union soldiers did not succumb to the panic they displayed at First Manassas.

At 10:00 P.M. Lee composed his victory message for Jefferson Davis: "This army achieved today on the plains of Manassas a signal victory over the combined forces of Gen[era]ls McClellan and Pope."[6] An effort the next day to cut off Pope's retreat resulted in a sharp firefight at Chantilly that was cut short by a soaking thunderstorm. John Pope was able to haul the sodden and defeated Army of Virginia behind Washington's defenses.

Any satisfaction Lee may have felt after thoroughly suppressing Pope was offset by an unlucky injury acquired on August 31. The general had been dismounted, talking with some officers in the woods, holding his reins loosely when a nearby cry of alarm spooked Traveler. Lee grabbed for the bridle and either tripped or was pulled off balance. As he fell, he used his arms to arrest the fall, taking most of the shock on his hands. A doctor was summoned who pronounced that Lee had broken a small bone in one hand and badly sprained the other. Splints for both were prescribed, so for the immediate future Lee would do his traveling in a wagon.

Jefferson Davis had barely savored Lee's victory announcement when a new message arrived. Dictating his note on September 3, Lee wasted no time getting to the point: "Mr. President: The present seems to be the most propitious time since the commencement of the war for the Confederate Army to enter Maryland."[7]

General Robert E. Lee's official correspondence was generally handled by his staff officers, Colonel A. L. Long and Major Walter H. Taylor. Following the second battle at Manassas, Lee kept both busy with a week of daily missives to Jefferson Davis explaining the dramatic course of action he was undertaking. At the same time, the steps Lee took underscored the gap between what he told the Confederate President and his actual intentions.

In this first and longest note, dated September 3, Lee itemized the principal reasons why he felt compelled to act. The two main Union armies in Virginia were at their lowest ebb, "much weakened and demoralized."[8] While fresh Northern troops were in the pipeline, they would not be available for field service for some time. It was not practicable for Lee to lay siege to Washington itself. Difficulties of keeping his army supplied and a lack of manpower sufficient to fully invest the enemy capital precluded it. Lee chose not to speak of other options available to him. He could pull back into the Shenandoah Valley, but that would surrender his hard-won initiative. Ditto withdrawing to the Rappahannock. As Lee saw it, he had no real option but to be bold.

In selling this proposal to Davis, Lee did not soft-pedal the problems. No one in their right mind would claim that his army was fully prepared for the rigors of a Maryland campaign. "It lacks much of the material of war, is feeble in transportation, the animals being much reduced, and the men are poorly provided with clothes, and in thousands of instances are destitute of shoes," said the general.[9]

Lee also suggested (as he would again in 1863) that with all the enemy's attention fixed on him, Richmond would be safe. Still, he urged Davis to do all in his power to bolster the city's defenses, and even bring in troops from the west to supplement the garrison.

Despite implying that his plans were still in a formative stage, Lee was well on his way toward concentrating his army around Leesburg, where it could access the upper Potomac's shallow fords. Also reaching him this day were 9,000 reinforcements sent by Davis in response to his earlier requests.

Without sharing any of his reasoning, Lee informed Davis on September 4 that he was more "fully persuaded" than ever of the necessity of raiding into Maryland and would so order "unless you should signify your disapprobation." Lee also offered the thought that having someone along who was well-known to Marylanders might smooth the way, so he had reached out to a former state governor sympathetic to the South's cause to see if he could join the expedition. (He either couldn't or wouldn't.) Lee also floated the possibility of continuing through Maryland into Pennsylvania, "unless you should deem it unadvisable upon political or other grounds."[10]

At the same time he was doing everything possible to prepare the army for the upcoming operation. He was appalled at the straggling he witnessed as the army concentrated at Leesburg, and he issued strict instructions to his brigade commanders to end it. He faced down a group of insubordinate soldiers, said to be mostly from the western Carolinas, who openly balked at taking the war into Northern territory. Lee had this small but rebellious band corralled and marched into the Shenandoah Valley, where they would be held until the army returned and they could rejoin their units. Also this day, portions of the Army of Northern Virginia began to cross the Potomac into Maryland via White's Ford.

As Lee described the scene for Davis on September 5, the Confederate army "is about entering Maryland." A new reason was proffered, namely, "affording the people of that State an opportunity of liberating themselves."[11] The rest of Lee's note concerned arrangements to be made to support the army when it returned from its expedition.

Far from "about entering" Maryland, the army's crossing of the Potomac went into high gear that day. As the men crossed the waist-deep water, bands on either bank serenaded them with endless repetitions of "Maryland, My Maryland."

Lee's briefest note of the series was dated September 6 and written "13 miles from Fredericktown, Maryland."[12] It announced that two divisions were across the Potomac. In fact, the first troops of Stonewall Jackson's wing entered Fredericktown that day. An onlooker was amazed "that this horde of ragamuffins could set our grand army of the Union at defiance."[13] More than one person in the crowd observed that for all their roughness of dress, Lee's soldiers kept their weapons in full working order.

A September 7 message to President Davis indicated that the Potomac crossing was completed and that the soldiers were being met with kindness by the civilians. Lee also had to admit that his hope of a heavy turnout of Maryland recruits was wishful thinking. "I do not anticipate any general rising of the people in our behalf," he stated.[14]

In a second, separate dispatch, he turned to the straggler problem, lamenting his lack of authority to deal forcefully with the matter. "We require more promptness [of court martials] and certainty of punishment," he fumed.[15] As he would make plain later in the war, Lee believed that the ultimate punishment—execution—was fully justified by the circumstances.

A proclamation to the people of Maryland was issued September 8 over Lee's signature. It claimed that the U.S. government was usurping the rights of Marylanders to decide their own destinies and offered service under Confederate arms as a remedy. It also promised to respect private property and individual rights.

In a pair of letters to Davis also transmitted September 8, Lee covered old and new ground. The old items provided a general summary of the army's current condition, intentionally vague in case of interception. The new subject stepped outside purely military matters by suggesting that the time was right for the South to call for peace negotiations with the North. Coming at a moment of great accomplishment for Southern arms, it would make a strong statement "that our sole object is the establishment of our independence and the attainment of an honorable peace."[16]

It was about this time that Lee learned of the most recent command shakeup in the Union armies. John Pope was out—no surprise there—replaced by Lee's old Peninsula nemesis, George B. McClellan. Major General John G. Walker, the officer in charge of some troops that had just arrived from Richmond, spoke with Lee at this time about his new/old opponent. "His is an able general, but a very cautious one," said Lee. "His army is in a very demoralized

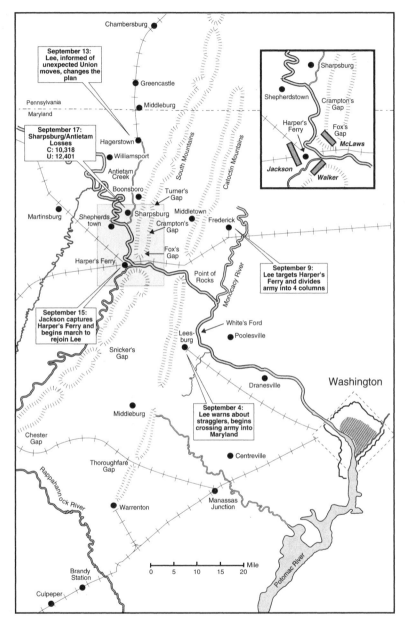

Chambersburg

September 13:
Lee, informed of
unexpected Union
moves, changes the
plan

Greencastle

Middleburg

Pennsylvania

Maryland

September 17:
Sharpsburg/Antietam
Losses
C: 10,318
U: 12,401

Hagerstown

Williamsport

Antietam
Creek

Boonsboro

Turner's
Gap

Martinsburg

Shepherds
town

Sharpsburg

Middletown

Crampton's
Gap

Frederick

Fox's
Gap

South Mountains

Catoctin Mountains

Harper's Ferry

Point of
Rocks

Monocacy River

September 9:
Lee targets Harper's
Ferry and divides
army into 4 columns

September 15:
Jackson captures
Harper's Ferry and
begins march to
rejoin Lee

White's Ford

Leesburg

Poolesville

Snicker's
Gap

Dranesville

Washington

Middleburg

September 4:
Lee warns about
stragglers, begins
crossing army into
Maryland

Chester
Gap

Centreville

Thoroughfare
Gap

Rappahannock River

Warrenton

Manassas
Junction

Potomac River

Brandy
Station

0   5   10   15   20   Mile

Culpeper

Inset map:

Sharpsburg

Shepherdstown

Crampton's
Gap

Harper's
Ferry

Fox's
Gap

McLaws

Jackson

Walker

SHARPSBURG/ANTIETAM CAMPAIGN

and chaotic condition, and will not be prepared for offensive operations—or he will not think it so—for three or four weeks."[17]

A letter from Jefferson Davis dated September 7 reached Lee two days from dispatch with the unwelcome news that the President, who was writing from near the Rapidan, proposed traveling to Leesburg, where he hoped to meet with his general. Lee hastened to disabuse Davis of the notion, citing risk of capture and the fact that Lee was breaking up his line of communication through the place. "I must therefore advise that you do not make an attempt that I cannot but regard as hazardous," he closed with finality.[18]

September 9 proved a day of dramatic decision for Lee. His intention from the beginning of the operation appears to have been to venture no farther east than Frederick (to appear to threaten either Washington or Baltimore), but then to draw back toward the west to reestablish his supply line to Richmond via the Shenandoah Valley. He would utilize the South Mountain range to limit the enemy's possible avenues of approach, thus luring McClellan into the open for the decisive battle denied him during the Seven Days.

There was a small problem. Once he had reached Frederick with his army, Lee fully expected that the small Federal garrisons astride the Shenandoah route would flee rather than risk capture. Most had, but two—Martinsburg and Harper's Ferry—had not. Lee decided that his first order of business was to clear them out of the way.

Speed was important, so Lee decided to employ overwhelming force to do the job. Assigning Stonewall Jackson to lead the expedition, Lee provided him with 26 of the 40 brigades available. This strike force would maneuver in three columns to converge on the targets in such a way as to block any escape by the garrisons. The remaining portion of the army, under Longstreet, would cover the rear of the enterprise just in case any Washington-based Union units tried to intervene. Stonewall was delighted with his semi-independent assignment, Longstreet greatly worried that so subdividing an army in the heart of enemy territory was asking for trouble. Lee shrugged off Longstreet's concerns and laid out the whole operation in Special Order No. 191, which was circulated to the various commanders involved.

The Army of Northern Virginia began the operation on September 10, with the portion under Longstreet the last to depart Frederick. It was Longstreet's job to cover the major South Mountain passes—south to north: Fox's Gap, Crampton's Gap, and Turner's Gap—but hardly had his men reached Boonsboro, their point of deployment, when Lee received a report that changed the plan. A Union column of unknown size had been spotted marching from Chambersburg, Pennsylvania, to Hagerstown, Maryland, which threatened Jackson's operation, something that could not be allowed to happen. Much to his dismay, Longstreet was told to forgo guarding the passes (cavalry plus one infantry division would do the job) in order to march at once to Hagerstown. With the ever-cautious McClellan in charge of the U.S. response, Lee remained sanguine and confirmed the change of mission.

The general reached Hagerstown on September 11, when he learned that the Union column advancing from Chambersburg was a figment of someone's imagination. He decided to hold Longstreet in the Hagerstown area until Jackson had finished with those pesky Yankee garrisons. The first inkling that affairs were not unfolding according to plan came during the late afternoon of September 13 when messages were received containing unexpected, unsettling news. Jeb Stuart, mainly responsible for Crampton's Gap, reported that the screening force he had spread across the eastern flank of the Catoctin Mountains had been shoved westward by the enemy. From D. H. Hill, whose division was watching over Turner's Gap, came news of a substantial number of Federal campfires visible near Middletown. Lee was puzzled but not panicked.

He was still pondering the meaning of this decidedly uncharacteristic behavior on McClellan's part when at about 10:00 P.M.

another rider brought him an additional Stuart dispatch. A reliable Confederate sympathizer from Frederick had ridden into the cavalry picket lines warning that the entire Federal army was stirring. Whatever assumptions Lee had made regarding McClellan's normally timid behavior had to be thoroughly reexamined.

He did some fast calculations. Still no word from Jackson about capturing Harper's Ferry. Having allotted so much of his force to this task, Lee was loath to call it off without more proof of serious trouble brewing. Jackson would be left to finish the job; however, Lee did warn one of the three columns involved in that operation (Major General Lafayette McLaws's), whose back was to Fox's Gap, of the increased threat level. Longstreet was instructed to march his troops at dawn back to Boonsboro to more closely support D. H. Hill.

A combination of anxiety and frustration prompted Lee to shed his invalid status on the morning of September 14 and take to riding Traveler once more, though his rein control was minimal. By midday it was becoming evident that significant combat was taking place for control of Crampton's and Turner's gaps. D. H. Hill called for help, which was promptly supplied by Longstreet. Because of his limited mobility, Lee made heavy use of his staff officers to monitor the situation.

With sunset came the realization that McClellan's army was present in all its strength, and while neither contested gap had been forced open, Lee had no realistic hope of still barring the door come morning. With Jackson and much of his army tied down on the Potomac's west side at Harper's Ferry, Lee was left with very few men to confront a suddenly aroused Yankee behemoth.

Lee was preparing to withdraw to the Potomac's west bank, and had even instructed McLaws to find his way into Virginia as best he could, when a note arrived from Jackson expressing his confidence that Harper's Ferry would soon fall. This was sufficient for Lee to change his mind. The withdrawal orders were cancelled and the troops under Longstreet were directed to concentrate at Sharpsburg, behind Antietam Creek.

September 15 was a time for fateful decisions. A midday courier reported Jackson's complete victory at Harper's Ferry, news Lee immediately relayed to the troops to cheer them. Jackson was instructed to march his men to Sharpsburg with the least delay. Throughout the daylight hours, the force under Lee's direct control—perhaps 15,000 men—took up defensive positions at Sharpsburg along with every cannon in Longstreet's arsenal. One of the soldiers recalled passing Lee and hearing him say, "We will make our stand on those hills."[19]

Lee still had no clue as to why McClellan was suddenly acting in such an animated fashion. Perhaps he imagined that pressure from Washington had forced his opponent to act with more alacrity than seen before; certainly Lee never considered the possibility that a copy of his Special Order No. 191 had fallen into McClellan's hands. That fact would not come to light for nearly a year, when the Union general's campaign report was released.

It was Lee's hope that after having uncharacteristically exerted himself storming the South Mountain passes, McClellan would revert to his former tepid behavior. Although forced by circumstances to assume a defensive posture, Lee's instincts remained fiercely offensive. Speaking about this moment after the war, Lee declared that "had McClellan continued his cautious policy for two or three days longer, I . . . would have had all my troops reconcentrated on [the] M[arylan]d side, stragglers up, men rested *& I intended then to attack McClellan.*"[20]

September 16 seemed to bear out Lee's reading of his opponent. The Union army, seemingly content just to observe, spread out to confront the Confederate position around Sharpsburg. Save for some random shelling, the entire martial tableau was eerily tranquil. Jackson arrived with commendable promptitude and his troops filed into positions Lee had chosen. The Army of Northern

Virginia remained three divisions short of a full compliment: Two were marching toward Sharpsburg, and one was tied down scouring Harper's Ferry for useful supplies and paroling the captured garrison. Still, Lee thought his cards remained well-hidden from his opponent. However, thanks to the intercepted orders McClellan knew approximately how much strength had been used against Harper's Ferry and how much was in front of him. That knowledge, plus the steady drumbeat from Washington to act, prompted McClellan to do what he had never managed to do on the Peninsula—order an attack. September 17 would be the day.

The dawn of what would enter the annals of the Civil War as its bloodiest single day of battle found Lee with perhaps 26,500 men of all arms on the field. Arrayed against him the Army of the Potomac began this day with some 65,000 on the firing line. Soon after sunrise the fighting began in earnest, and Lee exercised full control over his troops on the field. He was a constant presence to his men, calling forward reinforcements when needed and exhorting officers to hold their ground when no relief was on hand. Two of the three absent divisions that arrived soon after sunrise (upping Lee's strength by 10,000 muskets) were quickly sent into the maelstrom.

As Lee had anticipated, one of his greatest assets in this battle was McClellan himself, who utterly failed to take advantage of his substantial numerical superiority. Instead of pressing Lee's outnumbered force at various points along the four-mile line of battle, McClellan let it be fought in isolated segments—first against Lee's left flank, then his center, and finally against his right; allowing the general to shift troops from quiet areas to active ones in order to meet the attacks with something approaching parity.

Lee's combative mood was illustrated in one telling moment that afternoon when a mauled battery drew to a halt near him. The gunners had taken a terrible pounding, losing three of their four cannon and having witnessed their mangled comrades and horses.

When the officer in charge asked Lee for instructions, he was told to put the remaining piece back into action. Lee was approached by one of the begrimed cannoneers, who turned out to be his son, Robert Jr. "General, are you going to send us in again?" the boy soldier asked. Answered Lee: "Yes, my son, you all must do what you can to help drive these people back."[21]

Lee's fierce determination to prevail was matched by that of his soldiers, but by the end of this terribly long, terribly bloody day, even that did not seem to be enough. A late afternoon Federal breakthrough against Lee's right flank appeared to be on an unstoppable course to cut off access to Boteler's Ford, the only line of retreat, but it was halted by the timely arrival of the absent division hustling up from Harper's Ferry. At day's end, Lee and his army had survived.

The evening of September 17 Lee listened to reports from his officers and offered encouragement. When James Longstreet arrived Lee greeted him with words that became a sobriquet: "Ah, here is Longstreet; here is my old war horse."[22] The orders Lee issued this night prepared the army for another day of fighting. He had no intention of withdrawing from Sharpsburg until he was good and ready.

This time his reading of McClellan was spot on. September 18 passed with nothing more than outpost skirmishing and random cannon fire. Lee used the respite to evacuate the non-critically wounded, rest and resupply his men, and finish cleaning out Harper's Ferry. That night the rumble of wagons was constant. When daylight came, September 19, only the dead, dying, and desperately wounded held Sharpsburg. According to a story making the rounds, the one regimental band that tried to play the Johnny Rebs back across the Potomac with a rendition of "Maryland, My Maryland" was jeered to silence with shouts of "Maryland, *their* Maryland."

CHAPTER 9

Holding the Line

After successfully withdrawing his battered command across the
Potomac it was Lee's intention to quickly force McClellan into
another confrontation. Believing that his army needed only a
short rest to restore itself to combat readiness, he began formulat-
ing plans to ford the river at Williamsport in order to draw Mc-
Clellan toward him. A hard look at actual conditions gave pause
to Lee's ambitions. The number of men who had dropped out of
the ranks was far greater than he had imagined. Many of those
who had steadfastly stood beside their colors at Sharpsburg were
in something of a funk. A Southern reporter present recorded his
opinion that "the Confederate army was worn & fought to a perfect frazzle."[1]

Lee bowed to the inevitable on September 25. "I would not
hesitate to [renew the offensive] . . . even with our diminished

numbers," Lee explained to Davis, "did the army exhibit its former temper and condition; but, as far as I am able to judge, the hazard would be great and a reverse disastrous."[2] With the exception of another cavalry raid by Stuart that brought in some horses, positive headlines, and little else, the program for Lee's men became rest and refit.

The events at Sharpsburg assumed an importance on the larger world scene that Lee never imagined. In Washington on September 22, Abraham Lincoln used the Union victory as pretext to issue the preliminary Emancipation Proclamation. After January 1, 1863, all slaves held in Rebel territory were to be forever free. Overseas, British and French leaders backed off from plans under consideration to broker a North American peace. One of the pillars of Southern aspirations, foreign intervention, was gone; and the linchpin of its economy, the slave system, had been struck a dramatic blow.

Lee's daylight hours were filled with the minutiae of maintaining an army in the field at the end of an inadequate supply line. Supplies, shoes especially, arrived sporadically at best, and a lack of sufficient warm clothing did not bode well for the approaching winter. Rations rarely met minimum standards and Lee's complaints to Richmond were more often met with excuses than solutions.

Lee and Davis were able to enact some structural reforms within the army. The Confederate Congress approved the rank of lieutenant general along with the organization of units into army corps. Almost immediately Lee promoted Longstreet and Jackson, changing their wings into corps. Also added to the army's infantry roster was a number of slots for brigadier generals. Here Lee showed his political acumen by submitting a list of qualified candidates to Davis and allowing him to make the final appointments to insure proper state representation. Another recommendation to give Lee sufficient authority to weed out bad officers came through the legislative process as a half-measure that did not fully resolve the issue.

A bureaucratic battle Lee lost was a proposal to improve his artillery's performance by upgrading the commanding rank of the now-standard four-battery battalions from lieutenant colonel to brigadier general. With more of the battalions assigned directly to corps, he wanted the gunnery officers in charge to have sufficient authority to deploy the weapons on their own and not be subject to the whims of divisional or brigade commanders. When Jefferson Davis refrained from supporting the changes, Lee did a workaround by granting the battalion commanders the necessary authority without the rank.

Dark clouds gathered around the Lee clan. In the midst of his army restructuring in October, he received news that brought him to tears. One of his beloved children, 23-year-old Anne, had died in North Carolina after a brief illness. "To know that I shall never see her again on earth . . .," Lee commiserated to his wife, "is agonizing in the extreme."[3] Yet, such were the demands on him that except for occasional planning meetings in Richmond, Lee remained with the army.

His efforts began to bear fruit. By the beginning of November the Army of Northern Virginia numbered just over 70,000 strong. McClellan, who had obligingly left Lee unbothered during most of this period, finally began a ponderous movement toward Warrenton, Virginia. Carefully guarding against any surprises, the Union commander brought the Army of the Potomac to its destination by the end of October. Then, during the first week of November, McClellan was gone, removed from command by Lincoln for the last time. In his place was a general known to Lee by name only—Ambrose E. Burnside. "I fear they may continue to make these changes till they find some one whom I don't understand," Lee remarked to Longstreet upon receiving the news.[4] Then, on November 15, he learned that the enemy camps were stirring.

Several options were on the table. Burnside might be heading for an embarkation port on the Potomac to transfer his army to the James River, or he might be plotting a march along the eastern side of the Rappahannock. The river city of Fredericksburg could be his objective point. Lee hedged bets somewhat by sending a regiment with extra artillery there. Two days after the Federal army went into motion its vanguard was sighted approaching Falmouth, just north of Fredericksburg. Two of Longstreet's divisions were ordered to the Rappahannock town. Should the enemy cross the river in force in preparation for a march on Richmond, Lee had already picked out his best defensive line along the North Anna River. By November 20, he was more certain than ever that the Yankees were concentrating opposite Fredericksburg, so he transferred his headquarters there.

As the Union army gathered strength, Lee tried to read his opponent's mind. He was somewhat surprised that the Federals, having hustled to gain an advantage on him, now seemed content to wait. Lee used the respite to bring in more of his army, making the number present nearly 40,000 by the end of the month. Stonewall Jackson, holding station in the Shenandoah Valley, received orders on November 24 to march his corps to Fredericksburg. The last of Jackson's "foot cavalry" would complete the journey by December 3. Lee continued to wonder about Burnside's intentions. "What the designs of the enemy are I do not know," he confessed on November 28.[5]

The arrival of U.S. troops triggered an exodus of Fredericksburg civilians that was heartrending for the Rebel soldiers. Lucky citizens relocated to Richmond, while most quickly filled the few available spaces in nearby rural communities. Even lowly slave cabins became prime real estate commodities. Fredericksburg assumed the appearance of a ghost town.

Left to his own devices, Lee would not have selected the Fredericksburg area for a battle. The city itself was dominated by

Stafford Heights on Rappahannock's opposite bank, which the Federals could (and would) line with artillery. With easy access to the Potomac in their rear, the Union soldiers enjoyed a secure line of communication and supply. Lee's best defensive position was not in the city itself, but along a ridge crest just on its outskirts called Marye's Heights.

Longstreet's soldiers were distributed along this high ground and adjacent ridges, while Jackson's men extended the line southward. Lee just could not believe that the Federals intended to attack him at Fredericksburg, so even as the weather turned colder he would not allow the construction of winter quarters. By December 7 the nighttime temperatures were in the low 20s. The Army of Northern Virginia had reached full strength, with some 80,000 soldiers spread along Marye's Heights and beyond.

The enemy's move, when it came on December 11, was a surprise precisely because it wasn't a surprise. Instead of a flanking maneuver, Burnside's attack came head on. Preceded by a heavy bombardment and some bitter Fredericksburg street fighting, the Federals bulled their way across the Rappahannock, establishing footholds in the town itself and to the south, threatening an important road junction known as Hamilton's Crossing.

There was sharp scrapping for position on December 12 with the main Union effort coming the next day. December 13 saw intense fighting on both the Confederate right (Jackson's sector) and left (Longstreet's). The more wooded terrain on the right allowed some U.S. columns to penetrate and even disrupt portions of Jackson's line, but prompt counterattacks restored the status quo.

On the left, wave after wave of bluecoated infantry tramped up a wide open plain to assault Marye's Heights, and one by one they were shredded with terrible casualties. The slaughter wasn't all one way. Rebel soldiers had to move down the exposed slopes of the Heights to relieve their firing lines, taking heavy losses as they did so. Observing the martial display as the Union army deployed for battle, Lee commented: "It is well this is so terrible. We should grow too fond of it."[6] Even though he was watching events from high ground well behind the lines, Lee had two close calls; one when a nearby Rebel cannon burst and a large piece of it landed near him, the other when a Yankee shell hit in front of him but failed to explode. By day's end Union losses totaled 12,653 while the Army of Northern Virginia suffered 5,309 casualties, slightly higher on Longstreet's front than Jackson's.

Burnside's attack was a ghastly failure, but, as Lee had foreseen, there was nothing the Confederate army could do to exploit the situation. With the enemy's cannon dominating the river plain, no effort to drive the Federals into the Rappahannock could succeed. Jackson did organize a counterstroke, but cancelled it when he deemed the operation too costly. Writing on December 16 to his wife (the hand splints were off), Lee noted that Burnside's men "suffered heavily as far as the battle went, but it did not go far enough to satisfy me. . . . The contest will have to be renewed."[7]

Lee's capacity to keep his private and professional lives on discrete tracks was never more evident. Slightly more than two weeks after the Fredericksburg carnage, he finished compliance with one of the terms of his late father-in-law's will by emancipating the family slaves, at least 170 in total. The will had specified a five-year window for fulfilling the request; Lee had actually taken just a little longer. If he appreciated the irony of his little emancipation coming just days before Lincoln's larger one became official, he made no mention of it.

A false calm settled in as winter weather curtailed active operations. Lee used some of this down time to think about the Confederacy's chances to win this war and what might be done to improve them. He set down his thoughts in a January missive addressed to the newest secretary of war, James A. Seddon. Lee believed that he had come very close to winning the decisive victories that the Confederacy needed to survive. The critical factor limiting his success in every case was the lack of sufficient manpower. "More than once have most promising opportunities been lost for want of men to take advantage of them," wrote Lee, "and victory itself has been made to put on the appearance of defeat, because our diminished and exhausted troops have been unable to renew a successful struggle against fresh numbers of the enemy." No effort should be spared, he concluded, "to fill and maintain the ranks of our armies."[8]

Besides filling out his ranks, Lee was greatly worried about men emptying them. The conscription law that he had helped formulate proved a two-edged sword. While adding many more bodies to the army, it also swept up numbers of civilians whose devotion to the cause was decidedly less than total. The number of soldiers deserting their posts, while not epidemic, was serious enough to warrant resolute disciplinary actions. The new year witnessed a spate of firing squads carrying out Lee-approved court martial judgments against soldiers from Virginia, North Carolina, and South Carolina. After witnessing one such execution, a shaken surgeon expressed thoughts that doubtless reflected Lee's: "These severe punishments seem necessary to preserve discipline."[9]

If it all wasn't enough to vex a saint, Lee was the reluctant referee in what charitably might be called a difference of opinion between two of his three highest-ranking officers. It had all started in early September when Stonewall Jackson publicly reprimanded A. P. Hill for not marching his command with the requisite celerity. When Hill refused to acknowledge any wrongdoing, Jackson had him put under house arrest, still accompanying the army but not leading his division. The punishment was suspended during the Sharpsburg campaign, after which Hill pressed Lee for a formal hearing on the charges. Lee had a face-to-face with the pair that settled nothing. The two had been sniping at each other ever since, and once more Hill had appealed for adjudication. Another round of broadsides was exchanged, culminating with a request from

Jackson that Hill be reassigned. Lee could not figure out how to resolve this personnel problem and consequently did nothing.

Problems in distant places also vied for Lee's attention. A large Union raid into North Carolina in mid-December raised President Davis's anxiety level. Unlike Lee, who felt that maintaining strength to exploit opportunities in key battleground areas offset the temporary loss of less critical regions, the President always tried to respond to Federal thrusts anywhere along the Confederacy's perimeter. (As Lee stated the matter to another officer at this time, "Partial encroachments of the enemy we must expect, but they can always be recovered, and any defeat of their large army will reinstate everything.")[10] Lee repeated his concerns before releasing one division and the services of D. H. Hill, an able North Carolinian whose "queer temperament" (Lee's words)[11] had sorely tried his patience.

At a January 14 Richmond conference, Davis got Lee to commit two more brigades for North Carolina's defense and even schedule a visit to the threatened front. For once the unpredictable Burnside aided Lee's cause by suddenly putting his army in motion despite the bitter weather. Rushing back to Fredericksburg, Lee immediately suspended the transfer orders and cancelled his trip, while assuring Davis that if the President thought that the Tarheel State's present situation trumped the emergency on the Rappahannock he would let them go. Davis blinked.

A heavy snowstorm ended the Union movement without any combat. Davis's calls on Lee for troops put the general on notice that the stalemate along the Rappahannock made him liable to more such requests. He began making the case that a significant attack could be expected in Virginia this spring. "The enemy will make every effort to crush us between now and June," Lee argued, "and it will require all our strength to resist him."[12] He also had a new opponent to consider, for soon after his winter march fiasco, Ambrose Burnside was replaced by Major General Joseph Hooker.

Despite the dangers he anticipated on his front, Lee could not ignore the threat posed by the Union Ninth Corps, which, in mid-February, clambered aboard transports that steamed down the Potomac. Fretting over a thrust against his critical supply line running up through southeastern Virginia, Lee detached two divisions under Longstreet to counter the move.

Lee met with Jefferson Davis in Richmond in early March. The President wanted Longstreet to commence a more active campaign in the southeastern Virginia theater. Longstreet was willing, but only if he was heavily reinforced. Lee viewed Longstreet's detachment as only temporary, so he resisted pressures to entangle those troops in operations that might inhibit prompt recall. A sudden increase in the enemy's cavalry activities along the Rappahannock provided Lee sufficient cause to summon Longstreet, orders that he cancelled when the Union movement petered out.

This constant service was taking its toll on Lee, who too often relied on his natural stamina to see him through. After snapping at a loyal aide during one especially stressful period, Lee half-apologized: "Major Taylor, when I lose my temper, don't you let it make you angry."[13] He supplied more details about his physical condition in a letter to Mary penned that winter. "Old age & sorrow is wearing me away," he wrote, "& constant anxiety & labor, day & night, leaves me but little repose."[14] The onset of a "violent cold" in late March forced Lee to relinquish his tent headquarters for a warm room in a nearby house. Modern biographers diagnose this illness as the first sign of the cardiovascular deterioration that would eventually kill him.

The delicate juggling act that Lee was performing became even more difficult in late March when the U.S. Ninth Corps pulled up stakes in southeastern Virginia and was soon reliably reported to be on its way to Kentucky. Davis immediately sought to match the move by transferring Longstreet with his men to that distant front. Lee argued that it would be better for the Army of

Northern Virginia to move into the Shenandoah Valley, which would have the effect of drawing Hooker "out [of his entrenchments], or at least prevent further re-enforcements from being sent to the west."[15]

Lee's emphasis on offensive options was the logical extension of his reading of the political tea leaves. As he explained in a mid-April letter to his wife: "If [our operations are] successful this year, next fall there will be a great change in public opinion at the North. The Republicans will be destroyed & I think the friends of peace will become so strong as that the next administration will go in on that basis." As he saw it, the only way to achieve this objective was to continue "to resist manfully."[16]

Even as he and Davis sparred, the general quietly began laying plans for his second raid into northern states. Cartographer Jedediah Hotchkiss was commissioned to produce a series of route maps showing the roads as far north as Harrisburg, Pennsylvania, and even beyond that to Philadelphia.

Lee's timing was as much influenced by what the enemy did as it was by Davis's efforts to further disperse the Army of Northern Virginia. Davis himself was struggling through a series of ailments that sapped his energy and will. He had strength enough to argue with Lee but not enough to preemptively overrule him. While few army commanders would ever confess to hoping for a battle, it must have been with some small measure of relief that Lee notified Davis on April 29 that the enemy opposite him was on the march and a fight was imminent. Davis promptly set aside other considerations to begin orienting all available assets—Longstreet included—to the Rappahannock front.

The enemy's commencement of operations found Lee woefully unprepared in a number of critical areas. Still bedeviled by supply problems, he succumbed to temptation and allowed Longstreet to spread his two divisions throughout agriculturally rich southeastern Virginia to harvest badly needed foodstuffs. While this helped fill the larder, it created a new problem: It took those troops away from the railroad, where they were available for rapid transit when summoned, into the countryside, which added days to the recall response time. Lee accepted these risks in the full confidence that he would read the enemy's intentions early enough to react. This time he badly miscalculated.

Thus far he had faced Union commanders whose flaws worked to his advantage. McClellan's timidity, Pope's myopia, and Burnside's frustrated impulsiveness all contributed to his successes. Assuming that Joseph Hooker was cut from the same cloth was the kind of error that could kill an army. For instance, Lee knew from analyzing acquired Northern newspapers that his past opponents consistently overestimated the size of his army, and he assumed Hooker would do the same. In fact, among Hooker's innovations was the establishment of a professional intelligence-gathering operation that was providing him with remarkably accurate estimates of Lee's real strength and the locations of his units.

Lee also was counting on the enemy's poor morale and lackluster fighting spirit. Those same Northern papers carried stories about the short-term (two-year or nine-month) Yankee regiments due soon to muster out. Lee did not believe that such troops would count for much in a battle. The one lesson he seems not to have learned from the Peninsula, Sharpsburg, or even Second Manassas was that most Northern soldiers were as dedicated and obstinate in combat as his own men.

Perhaps most fatally, Lee did not credit his opponent with having smarts equal to his own. He was certain he could quickly ferret out anything the enemy tried to do. So when a Confederate signal station deciphered a coded Federal flag message indicating that the Yankee cavalry was heading into the Shenandoah Valley, Lee took it at face value and promptly positioned his own mounted units to intercept the Federals. The result was to separate his cavalry from his infantry by some twenty miles. This was an even better result than Hooker had imagined when he arranged for the deceptive signal to be sent using a code known to have been cracked by the Rebels.

This time, Lee's pattern of calculated risks, coupled with a self-assurance bordering on overconfidence, was placing his entire army in dire jeopardy.

━┿═══┿━

The enemy confronting Lee at Fredericksburg suddenly came alive on April 29. In a series of well-planned actions, a pair of Federal divisions crossed the Rappahannock at two places about two miles south of Fredericksburg and immediately fortified a bridgehead. If Lee was worried he took care not to show it. "I thought I heard firing," he remarked to the staff officer delivering the report, "and was beginning to think it was about time some of you young fellows were coming to tell me what it was all about."[17] As the Yankees seemed content to rest on their laurels, Lee, still wary of the enemy artillery along Stafford Heights, merely observed the Union soldiers industriously digging in.

Another piece of the developing puzzle was presented to Lee at midday when a courier brought a dispatch from Jeb Stuart reporting that some Union cavalry, infantry, and artillery were pushing over the Rappahannock at Kelly's Ford, perhaps 25 miles northwest. From a captured staff officer Stuart identified the force as Hooker's Eleventh Corps and its probable destination as Gordonsville. Given all the data in hand this made sense to Lee, who assumed that the raiders were a diversion, with the real effort to be a turning movement below Fredericksburg.

Lee had to admit that General Hooker had done a good job masking his build-up of troops. The infantry reinforcements Lee had summoned would be days in coming. Worse yet, because his artillery battalions had to forage for their animals he had permitted them to disperse into camps further south. It would take these gunners long hours, if not days, to reach him. Lee acknowledged as much that evening when he told Jefferson Davis of the day's events, adding: "Our scattered condition favors their operation."[18]

More intelligence arrived near dusk from pickets posted along the Rapidan River who saw some Union cavalry and a few infantry. This portended a raid on the army's rear. Lee quickly ordered a pair of brigades from Richard Anderson's division camped near Chancellorsville to establish security roadblocks.

Even if Lee wasn't sure where the blow was coming from, he was increasingly certain that this was the big one. Something of his urgency slipped into his admonition to the officer commanding the troops confronting the Yankee bridgehead when he urged him to tell his soldiers "that it is a stern necessity now, it must be Victory or Death, for defeat would be ruinous."[19]

Lee battled chest pains on the morning of April 30, even as he continued to scrutinize the jigsaw puzzle. More information from Jeb Stuart raised the stakes considerably by identifying at least three Union corps now along the Rapidan. Lee ordered two of his most able engineers to help Anderson lay out a defensive line and routed some extra artillery there, too. Anderson was urged to set all his "spades to work as vigorously as possible."[20]

When he felt well enough to ride, Lee viewed the Yankee lodgment below Fredericksburg in the company of Stonewall Jackson, who was all for attacking. The enemy's artillery dominance of the river valley made it easy for Lee to turn Jackson down.

Lee returned to his headquarters, reviewed all the information in hand, and rode back to resurvey the Federal position south of the town. The fact that no effort was being made to further reinforce or expand the pocket, coupled with the increasing evidence of large-scale activity in the Chancellorsville vicinity, finally convinced him that General Hooker had cleverly kept him looking at one hand while the other did the trick. According to staff officer

Charles Marshall, Lee snapped his telescope shut with the comment, "The main attack will come from above."[21]

Characteristically, once he had reached a conclusion his quick mind enabled him to jump to a plan of action. Orders went out directing more than four-fifths of his available force to march to Chancellorsville, with McLaws's division followed by Jackson's Corps. Two could play the Yankee game at Fredericksburg. Lee would leave behind just one division under Major General Jubal Early (perhaps 12,400 men altogether) to keep the Federals penned in place. Lee's intention, as he outlined to Richmond, was to "hold our lines in rear of Fredericksburg with part of the force and endeavor with the rest to drive the enemy back to the Rapidan."[22]

On the morning of May 1, Stonewall Jackson demonstrated how much Lee's trust in him was justified. Operating under necessarily vague instructions "to repulse the enemy," Jackson aggressively pushed his columns forward to contact.[23] The resultant combat, kept close to the roads by the heavily wooded terrain, proved a serious psychological shock for Joseph Hooker. His plan, which up to this point had gone almost flawlessly, assumed brushing aside light picket screens on these roads, but the soldiers in his vanguard were fighting heavy infantry columns.

In a grand tactical sense the Union army may have still possessed the initiative, but doubts were sprouting in Hooker's mind, while Lee's sense of purpose was crystalline in its clarity. Vanguard fought vanguard on the limited pathways throughout the day with little rhyme or reason to the struggle save its deadly constancy. Perhaps 600 men fell on both sides, but at day's end Joseph Hooker believed he could best win this battle by going over to the defensive and so ordered his troops back into a perimeter around Chancellorsville.

Robert E. Lee sat down at dusk with Stonewall Jackson on a fallen log in a woods clearing near the intersection of the Orange Plank and Catharine Furnace roads. Lee biographer Clifford

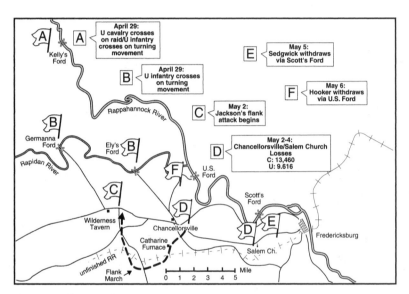

CHANCELLORSVILLE

Dowdey masterfully sketched the moment: "Both wore long double-breasted gray coats and high boots. Lee's gray felt hat with the brim slightly curved at the sides sat squarely on his head, and Jackson's battered [V.M.I.] cadet cap perched over his eyebrows."[24] Jackson opined that Hooker would withdraw now that his gambit had been exposed. Lee wasn't so sure. He was still guided by the simple objective: How can we get at those people?

He enjoyed one advantage given him by his opponent. Hooker's plan to baffle the Confederates was too clever by half. He had dispatched most of his cavalry on a sweeping raid to the west and south, expecting it would further divide the enemy's forces. Lee barely took the bait, allowing just two mounted regiments to chase after the interlopers. The rest of the Rebel cavalry, led by Jeb Stuart, dominated the road systems south and west of Chancellorsville, so anything the Confederates did there would be undetected.

Lee's first order of business was to collate all the known data and to fill in any critical blanks. A rough picture of the enemy's position emerged. Early in the discussion Lee considered and then rejected the idea of attacking the enemy's left near the Rappahannock. That flank was tightly buttoned down. Lee remarked to Jackson that "we must attack on our left as soon as possible."[25]

Lee never wavered in his determination to resume the offensive and now he had the point of attack. As often happens in such situations, once a decision was made, needed information began to accumulate. Cavalry scouts reported the Yankees were thin about two miles west of Chancellorsville, meaning their flank was in the air. The chaplain on Jackson's staff was a local who knew the area roads. He said there was a way for a column of troops to work across the Yankee front to get around their flank west of Chancellorsville. Any lingering doubts were gone now, and Lee went to bed fully aware of what the morning would bring.

Lee and Jackson were up early on May 2 working out the final details of the flank attack. Jackson had had his chaplain sketch out the route on his map and after examining it the general said he was uncomfortable with one stretch that seemed too close to the enemy's position. The cleric remembered a neighbor whose knowledge of the local byways surpassed his own, so, accompanied by Jackson's cartographer Major Jedediah Hotchkiss, they rode two miles to question the man. He did indeed know his way through the woods and provided the information Jackson was seeking along with a bonus shortcut or two.

Returning to camp, Hotchkiss shared his discoveries with Lee and Jackson, who were sitting on discarded U.S. hardtack boxes. The two generals were satisfied that the final element of the plan was now in place. Almost like a school teacher reinforcing a lesson, Lee closed out the discussion with a recap.

"Well, General Jackson," he said, "what do you propose to do?"

Jackson traced the agreed upon route on the map. "I propose to go right around there," he said.

"What do you propose to do it with?"

"With my whole command."

"What will you leave me here to hold the Federal army with?"

"The two divisions that you have here."

Lee did the math. Jackson would be taking perhaps two-thirds of the army with him. The risk, if the enemy figured out what was happening and fell upon the one-third with Lee, would be catastrophic. Most commanders would have hedged their bets by weakening the flanking force, but Lee knew that for the plan to deliver the kind of victory he sought it had to be strong. All this took a few seconds.

"Well, go ahead," Lee said.[26]

<hr />

There were some things that even Stonewall Jackson could not hurry. Getting a corps in camp to accelerate from zero to marching speed took several hours. It was nearly 7:00 A.M. before his leading elements tramped off into the wilderness. For a while Lee watched them go. He was joined briefly by Jackson. The two shared some private words and then Stonewall too was gone.

Having made what was perhaps the most momentous battle-field decision of his military career, Lee next tackled some lesser ones. The Fredericksburg front had been quiet all this time, prompting Lee to wonder if Jubal Early's muskets might be better employed helping him should the Yankees cause trouble before Jackson struck. He called in his chief-of-staff, Colonel Robert Chilton, and explained his instructions. If Early believed that the Federals at Fredericksburg posed no real danger, he was to leave a small holding force in place and march the rest to Lee. Chilton departed with the message. Lee turned to other matters.

Jackson's departure created some gaps in the Confederate defensive alignment, requiring Lee to move some of the remaining brigades to fill the holes. He further instructed the pickets to keep up an active—but not too active—fire. He wanted to discourage enemy probes, not bring on a firefight that might flare out of control.

Lee also used this long pause between acts to send a note to Jefferson Davis reviewing the situation to date. Just in case his plan did not work out, Lee warned the President that he would "have to fall back and Fredericksburg must be abandoned."[27] If that happened, it would be crucial for him to have Longstreet's missing two divisions, so Lee emphasized the need to keep those men moving north.

Shortly after midday semi-serious gunfire was heard near Catharine Furnace, a place along Jackson's march route. A strong Union reconnaissance detachment probing that area encountered a Georgia regiment left there to guard against that very contingency. Lee quickly pushed out some regiments to lend a hand, while several of Jackson's trailing units reversed course to assist. The Yankees scored some points by enveloping most of the unfortunate Georgia regiment, but then misread the flank movement as a retreat and pulled back.

Likely after 4:00 P.M. Lee received a message written in Jackson's hand reporting that he had reached the enemy flank and would attack "as soon as practicable." It closed with a supplication to God for "great success."[28] Lee replied to Jackson, assuring him that the moment his guns opened, he would press the lines in his front.

Battle plans may be well considered and made under reasonable assumptions, but there is a human factor that can render even the most astute calculations null and void. There was nothing exceptional about the orders Lee sent to Jubal Early; in fact, they repeated instructions already given on May 1. However, in the process of explaining it to Early, Colonel Chilton got it wrong. Rather than a discretionary order, he delivered it as a peremptory one; no matter what the situation at Fredericksburg, Early was to march the bulk of his command to reinforce Lee.

The feisty division commander sputtered some unprintable words but did as he was told. It was likely the confirmation he sent Lee of his actions that first alerted the general that his instructions had been garbled through what he later termed "a misapprehension on the part of the officer conveying" it.[29] Lee immediately sent a clarification to Early and hoped for the best.

It was not long after 5:30 P.M. when the sporadic musketry off to the west crescendoed to the roar of a full-fledged battle. Jackson was launching his attack. Lee ordered the two divisions with him to make a noisy demonstration and he personally directed several companies of a Virginia regiment to fake a charge. Throughout this dangerous charade, Lee made certain that the basic defensive lines he was holding were never compromised.

For hours Lee's only monitoring of Jackson's action was by the sound of his guns. Finally, around midnight, the spiteful rumblings died away. With nothing to do until word came from Jackson, Lee made a rough bed on the ground and snatched some needed rest.

May 3 was only about three hours young when Robert E. Lee woke up after hearing his staff officers talking with a messenger from Jackson. Lee called for the man, Captain Robert E. Wilbourn, Jackson's signal officer. He listened intently as the young man described the dramatic march and fight, which had ended in a significant victory. There was more. Jackson had been wounded toward the end of the engagement while reconnoitering the confused battle lines. Wilbourn was of the opinion that the wound was not mortal.

"Thank God it is not worse," Lee interjected. "God be praised that he is yet alive."[30] After a moment's reflection he added, "Ah, Captain, any victory is dearly bought which deprives us of the services of General Jackson, even for a short time!"[31]

Wilbourn ran down a short list of other senior officers who had been hit in the attack and noted that the ranking major general on the scene, Jeb Stuart, presently commanded the corps. Lee announced to his staff, "These people must be pressed today."[32] He dictated a message to Stuart emphasizing that the job was not finished. Lee urged the cavalryman to "let nothing delay the completion of the plan of driving the enemy from his rear and from his positions."[33]

A second messenger from the west reached Lee about a half hour after Wilbourn. It was the reliable Jedediah Hotchkiss, who brought a map. From it Lee could see that little more than a mile separated the troops with him from those under Stuart, with a mass of the enemy interposed at a place called Hazel Grove. Linking hands became Lee's principal objective. Stuart was instructed to press hardest on his right, while Lee worked troops to his left. There would be more combat that day around Chancellorsville.

It was not long after 7:00 A.M. when the sounds of battle once more grumbled and roared. Lee functioned as a division commander, doing all he could to keep the lines pressing forward. The contest was in close, personal and savage. Finally, a little after 10:00 A.M., the Federals fell back to a new defensive line, leaving Hazel Grove and Chancellorsville in Rebel hands. Lee's army was whole again. He hurried to Chancellorsville. Almost as soon as the infantrymen recognized him they began to cheer. Lee, recorded staff officer Charles Marshall, "sat in the full realization of all that soldiers dream of—triumph."[34] He waved his hat to acknowledge the cheering.

A messenger intercepted Lee with a note from the wounded Jackson formally transferring command and congratulating Lee on the victory. Lee's prompt reply returned the credit to Jackson along with instructions for him to be moved to a more secure location. Barely had orders been given for Stuart to halt long enough to regroup his scattered formations when Lee was handed an urgent note. Matters at Fredericksburg had gone from bad to worse. Even though Early had successfully reoccupied his abandoned lines, he had placed most of his strength where he felt most vulnerable, on the southern end of his position. His Union opponent, Major General John Sedgwick, piled on the relatively few defenders holding Marye's Heights and carried it, forcing Early to fall back to the southwest.

While Lee's decision to order Jackson's flank march is often touted as his greatest battlefield accomplishment, his course of action after learning of the Fredericksburg fiasco runs a close second. Barely skipping a beat, Lee decided to suspend further attacks against the Yankees at Chancellorsville—for now—and confront this fresh crisis. Stuart's troops would maintain an active presence to keep Hooker guessing while Lee directed McLaws to take the three brigades with him (a fourth was already at Fredericksburg) to resolve the crisis. Lee soon added a brigade from Richard Anderson's division, which, like those of McLaws's, had not been heavily engaged this day.

For two hours, beginning around 5:00 P.M. Lee could hear the sound of fighting to his rear. Messages kept him apprised of the changing situation. What was clear was that McLaws had halted the Federal advance near a place called Salem Church. Just stopping it wasn't good enough for Lee; if he couldn't get at Hooker behind his earthworks, he would settle for the piece of the Union army that was out in the open. A stream of messages from his headquarters to Early and McLaws sought to coordinate a converging attack at first light. "It is necessary that you beat the enemy," Lee told McLaws, "and I hope you will do it."[35]

With other officers requesting instructions about various matters, it was well past midnight before Lee could manage some rest.

Lee had to assume that Hooker had some knowledge of what Major General John Sedgwick, commanding the Federal breakout, was doing. A junction of those two commands would spell big trouble for Confederate aspirations. Keeping Hooker on tenterhooks would forestall that, so Lee authorized some creative harassment. At three in the morning, May 4, a detail of artillery quietly unlimbered on a piece of open ground overlooking the river and executed a surprise bombardment of the Yankee camps near U.S. Ford. In addition, a few planted deserters spread stories that Longstreet's men were at hand. Neither the shock fusillade nor the fake stories panicked Hooker, but valuable time and attention was spent sorting out fact from fiction. The payoff came late that day when a coordinated attack was unleashed against Sedgwick's position, now a south-facing semi-circle with both flanks on the Rappahannock, and Hooker provided only a modicum of lukewarm moral support.

Sedgwick had to be quickly eliminated, before Hooker wised up, yet it seemed to Lee that his lieutenants did not grasp the urgency. In response to an early morning request for more troops to assist, Lee released three additional brigades from Anderson (leaving just three divisions to make sure Hooker stayed put) and then rode to Salem Church, reaching McLaws's headquarters shortly before midday.

Lee saw at once that the officers were not working together; each was puzzling over his own piece while no one exercised any overall authority. Lee went hands on. He ordered out scouts to pin down the enemy's exact location, directed Rebel units into jump-off positions, and at 6:00 P.M. watched the attack get underway. By nightfall the Federal perimeter had been dented but not cracked.

Lee's men were bone tired, but such was his anxiety to finish off Sedgwick before Hooker caught on that he ordered a risky night attack. Hastily organized advances stumbled onto Federal units already pulling back into tighter defensive positions, so while some additional ground was occupied, no tactical advantage was gained.

Soon after sunrise, May 5, Lee learned that Sedgwick had successfully evacuated his entire command over the Rappahannock. As soon as initial reports were confirmed, Lee ordered Fredericksburg reoccupied and then turned his attention back to Hooker near Chancellorsville.

Once more barely breaking stride, Lee revived his plan to drive the Yankees back into the river. He immediately began arranging his forces for a simultaneous strike against both enemy flanks. The weary fighters of McLaws and Anderson marched to Chancellorsville to complete Lee's battle line. However, a higher power intervened. Beginning about 4:00 P.M. heavenly sluices opened as rain came down and kept coming. Lee (perhaps reluctantly since a rise in the river might have trapped Hooker on the Rebel side) postponed the assault until the next morning.

Lee awoke early to begin issuing the necessary attack orders. In the midst of this activity he was interrupted by one of his subordinate commanders, Brigadier General Dorsey Pender, who informed him that the Yankees had evacuated, slipped back across the Rappahannock during the night. Lee could not believe that no one had heard Hooker's army take its leave. "Why, General Pender!" he sputtered. "That is the way you young men always do. You allow those people to get away. I tell you what to do, but you don't do it!" Pender had no excuses to offer. Lee dismissed him. "Go after them," he snapped impatiently, "and damage them all you can!"[36]

The enemy had been stopped in its designs, but it had cost the Army of Northern Virginia almost one man in four to do so. Forced to react to Hooker's moves, Lee had used every available asset to restore the situation to what it was before the Yankee operation began. This left him more convinced than ever that waiting to see what the enemy did first was a strategy sure to fail in the long run.

+≍≍⊹+

Shortly before 3:15 P.M., May 10, Stonewall Jackson died from wounds received at Chancellorsville. He had survived the amputation of his left arm and seemed to be recovering when pneumonia took hold and inexorably began killing him. Lee had been kept regularly briefed throughout the ordeal as his able lieutenant's health rallied and then faltered. "God will not take him from us, now that we need him so much," he exclaimed after one report. To a chaplain Lee admitted that he had "wrestled in prayer for him . . . as I never prayed, I believe, for myself."[37]

Heading the list of unfinished business on Jackson's death was his dispute with A. P. Hill, which now would never be adjudicated. Throughout Jackson's final confinement he had been visited by a number of friends, family, and officers, but not Lee. The commander of the Army of Northern Virginia had just directed a series of battles that left 1,724 of his men killed, 9,233 wounded, and 2,503 missing. Still he had to keep distance between himself and the one among that number he most valued. Lee limited briefings on Jackson's condition with the comment that "it is too painful a subject."[38]

Announcing Jackson's passing, Lee had only words of praise for the "daring, skill and energy of this great and good soldier."[39] The plain fact was that Jackson completed Lee. As he said of his lieutenant on a previous occasion: "I have but to show him my design, and I know that if it can be done it will be done."[40] All that Lee could do now was to file the pain away and move on. Words he said to one chaplain while Jackson still clung to life summed it best: "He has lost his left arm, but I have lost my right."[41]

An image of Lee at the time of the Mexican War, a young officer of great promise.

Mary Anna Randolph Custis Lee (1807–1873) around 1838.

Lee at Chancellorsville, from a painting by H. A. Ogden. The soldiers greeted him with tremendous cheers.

An allegorical image of Lee at the grave of Stonewall Jackson that appeared before 1870. Said Lee in 1863: "He has lost his left arm, but I have lost my right."

A postwar image centered on (left to right) Stonewall Jackson, P. G. T. Beauregard, and Lee. A constellation of other Confederate leaders surrounds the trio.

An idealized lithograph (above) showing the moment during the Battle of Spotsylvania (May 13, 1864) when Lee personally attempted to lead reinforcements into combat.

Below: Lee as a Southern symbol in a postwar image that was packaged with tobacco products.

A photograph of Robert E. Lee likely taken in 1864 by the Richmond photographer J. Vannerson.

Lee's dignified General Orders No. 9 announcing the surrender to his troops transformed into a gaudy broadside a few years after his death.

Lee after the war, a photograph likely made in Lexington shortly before he embarked on his "farewell" tour.

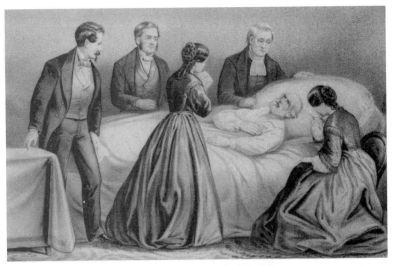

Above: Lee was one old soldier who definitely did not just fade away. This Currier & Ives lithograph appeared soon after Lee's passing.

Left: Artist Thomas Nast's imagining of Lee waiting in the McLean House for Grant to arrive. The painting was remained unfinished when Nast died in 1902.

CHAPTER 10

Raiding North (2)

Little more than a week after Chancellorsville, Lee returned to Richmond for another strategy session with Jefferson Davis. A War Department clerk named John B. Jones who encountered him on May 15 thought the general appeared "thinner, and a little pale."[1] Lee was now something of a celebrity following his hard-fought victories at Second Manassas, Fredericksburg, and Chancellorsville. Newspapers hailed him "as one of the great military masters."[2]

It was ironic that, in some important ways, Lee's "victory" at Chancellorsville presented him with greater problems than would have a defeat. He had prevailed with almost 16,000 of his army on detached service. To some this suggested that these soldiers might be better utilized elsewhere in the Confederacy. And, as it turned out, there was another military front then in desperate need of more Southern fighting men.

It was Vicksburg, Mississippi, the Mississippi River fortress city holding open the door to the Confederacy's western states. Vicksburg's defenders had already withstood several attacks by Federal land and naval forces. Yet another campaign was underway, but this time the prognosis was grim. On May 14 Richmond officials learned that Vicksburg's vital inland link, the city of Jackson, had fallen to Union forces under a general named Grant. Reinforcements were so urgently needed that Secretary of War James Seddon wondered if the Army of Northern Virginia could not spare some. Even before Chancellorsville, Seddon proposed to Lee that he release "two or three brigades" to be combined with others to create "an encouraging re-enforcement to the Army of the West."[3]

Lee did not directly oppose Seddon's request; he merely pointed out all the things that could go wrong with such a complicated transfer of soldiers. Then the Army's adjutant and inspector general added his bit, raising the request to a full division. Lee counterproposed that he make an aggressive move into the North, sure to attract the enemy's potential western reinforcements. The Chancellorsville operation interrupted this exchange.

Just two days after the fighting ended, Lee resumed the dialogue. He pointed everyone's attention further south where General P. G. T. Beauregard commanded Confederate forces defending the Atlantic coast from South Carolina to Florida. Lee argued that the summer swamp fevers common to the low-lying region would keep the Federals inactive, and suggested that Beauregard's troops might be better employed closer to Richmond. That would free up units Lee wanted so they could be returned to him.

When that scenario did not convince Seddon, Lee prophesied disaster. Reducing his army's size, he said, would force him to relinquish the Rappahannock line and fall back on Richmond, thus abandoning much of northern Virginia to the enemy. President Jefferson Davis, who was monitoring the discussion, intervened with the opinion that it was "just such an answer as he expected from Lee, and he approves it. Virginia will not be abandoned."[4]

Lee met with Davis and Seddon throughout the afternoon of May 15. No one kept any notes. He likely used words that he would use again, explaining that an "invasion of the enemy's country breaks up all of his preconceived plans, relieves our country of his presence, and we subsist while there on his resources."[5] Lee doubtless renewed his claim to Major General George E. Pickett's division, then on loan to Richmond's defenses. Seddon would have repeated his concern about the growing crisis at Vicksburg and the imperative need to redirect scarce manpower assets.

Although he was still recuperating from a recent illness, Jefferson Davis did not hold back from the discussion. Initially, as Lee much later recalled, "Mr. Davis did not like the [prospect of the] movement northward." The Confederate President feared for Richmond's safety if its principal shield were to be removed. Lee countered that "by concealing his movements and managing well, he could get so far north as to threaten Washington before they could check him, & this once done he knew there was no need of further fears about their moving on Richmond." With his army in motion, Lee was confident he could "baffle and break up" any enemy schemes.[6] In the end, Jefferson Davis bought Lee's arguments. Lee could reinforce his army for a northward advance.

Having won his point, Lee was elsewhere when Davis called in his full cabinet on May 16 to rehash the matter. The army commander did not have to be present. War Department clerk John B. Jones knew immediately who had won as he watched the "long column" of Pickett's division marching "through the city northward," even as the cabinet revisited the matter. "Gen. Lee," Jones noted, "is now stronger than he was before the battle [of Chancellorsville]."[7] When Lee paid a social call that evening he seemed renewed. A young man sighting him never forgot the "superb figure of our hero" and thought Lee the "most noble looking mortal I had ever seen."[8]

Lee typically did not reveal his full hand. At the worst, a march into Maryland and beyond would considerably alleviate his logistical situation. But by taking his army into the enemy's breadbasket Lee could help himself to a rich larder of livestock, grains, and a large ambiguous category of goods euphemistically termed "military supplies." Also, by taking the point of battle away from northern Virginia, he would allow Old Dominion farmers to harvest their summer crops free of enemy interference.

There was an even more important reason to move north. While a later generation of writers would tout Chancellorsville as "Lee's greatest victory," it is clear that its principal architect did not see it that way. His post-battle proclamation had termed the results a "glorious victory"; but those kind of statements demanded such language. More likely, Lee would have agreed with the reporter covering the campaign for the *Richmond Enquirer:* "I believe General Lee expected a more brilliant result."[9] Reviewing the results with an aide sent by President Davis, Lee concluded that while the Confederate "loss was severe," the net result was that "we had gained not an inch of ground and the enemy could not be pursued."[10]

He had taken great risks with his army at Chancellorsville. His goal throughout was not merely to drive the enemy force back across the Rappahannock River, but to destroy it as a military force. In the next campaign he hoped to find the battle of annihilation he had failed to manage at Chancellorsville. All other reasons proffered for his intended operation were secondary. According to the recollection of a staff officer, Lee "knew oftentimes that he was playing a very bold game, but it was the only *possible* one."[11]

Lee had won the bureaucratic trench fight, but just for the moment. He worried that the next dawn would bring news from the west that might upset everything. As he left Richmond on May 18 Lee knew for certain he would have to act quickly. Still, the prospect of achieving his long-sought goal was a tonic. On his way to rejoin his army, Lee breakfasted with a family friend who was "very glad to see that the great and good man was so cheerful."[12]

Immediately after returning from Richmond, Robert E. Lee reorganized his army from two infantry corps to three. As he explained to Jefferson Davis, the old arrangement with each corps numbering about 30,000 muskets represented "more than one man can properly handle & keep under his eye in battle."[13] A new Third Corps was created by taking a division apiece from the First and Second Corps, and adding a new division cobbled together from various unattached units.

There were other important changes. The artillery battalions (four batteries each) were assigned to corps; no longer were they dispersed down to the brigade level. Those not attached to corps were part of an artillery reserve. While not reorganized to any degree, Lee's cavalry corps was increased in size with the addition of six regiments and a battalion.

Jackson's death necessitated a fresh leadership team. Lee met with his key lieutenants on June 1. His anchor in the reorganized army was Lieutenant General James Longstreet, whose First Corps retained most of its old units. Longstreet could be counted on to be blunt in his assessments and cautious in his tactics. While Lee thought he had the measure of the man, he likely underestimated his subordinate's ambitions.

The Army of Northern Virginia's revamped Second Corps was essentially Jackson's old command. For its leader Lee tapped Virginian Richard Stoddert Ewell, a forty-six-year-old professional officer who had served with distinction under Jackson, suffering a wound that cost him his left leg in August 1862 fighting near Manassas. Lee termed Ewell "an honest, brave soldier, who had always done his duty well."[14] Privately, however, he worried that

Ewell was subject to periods of "quick alternations from elation to despondency."[15]

The new Third Corps was headed by Ambrose Powell Hill, a thirty-seven-year-old Virginian whose reputation as a hard fighter applied both on and off the battlefield. His long public wrangle with Jackson had not been forgotten after Stonewall's death. For a short while a malicious rumor circulated that Jackson had used some of his last words to blackball Hill as his successor. In Lee's opinion, A. P. Hill was simply "the best soldier of his grade with me."[16]

All this was just part of the transformation that Lee completed in record time. Of the nine infantry divisions in the new scheme, a third were led by men untried at that level, and out of thirty-seven brigades with the nine divisions, thirteen were entrusted to officers with no previous command experience. At any other juncture such wholesale changes would have required an extended shakedown period before the army was committed to a major campaign. Lee could not wait.

The pressure was on Lee to complete his labors before events elsewhere intruded, and as a result his normally patient diplomacy and tact began to wear thin. Two days before meeting with his corps commanders, he fired off a pair of peevish notes to Richmond. He complained to Jefferson Davis that D. H. Hill in North Carolina had refused his request to release troops promised him. This action, Lee fumed, so compromised his situation that should the Federal army again come at him, there "may be nothing left for me to do but fall back [toward Richmond]." To Secretary of War Seddon, Lee griped that some of the troop transfers that D. H. Hill had approved were administrative smoke screens. An experienced brigade in Pickett's division had been replaced by a makeshift one that in turn had been dispersed back to its original commands, leaving Pickett a brigade short. "I . . . dislike to part with officers & men who have been tried in battle and seasoned to the hardships of the campaign in exchange for wholly untried troops," Lee repined.[17]

However, he took out none of these frustrations on his corps commanders. It is unlikely that he gave them any specific orders beyond designating routes for the first stage of the coming movement. Of the campaign's overall shape, Longstreet recollected it thus: "The enemy would be on our right flank while we were moving north. Ewell's Corps was to move in advance to Culpeper Court House, mine to follow, and the cavalry was to move along on our right flank to the east of us. Thus by threatening his rear we could draw Hooker from his position . . . opposite Fredericksburg."[18] Most of Lee's army would enter the Shenandoah Valley, taking full advantage of the Blue Ridge Mountains to screen its right flank. In a communication sent to Richmond on June 2, Lee gave the impression that he had not yet decided whether or not to advance. Said Lee, "if I am able to move, I propose to do so cautiously, watching the result, and not to get beyond recall until I find it safe."[19]

With Hooker's army camped just over the Rappahannock, Lee began to gingerly ease his army away from Fredericksburg beginning on June 3. He did so even though all the troops promised him from Richmond had yet to arrive. Arguing for their return would become a regular feature of Lee's communications back to Richmond, though, for a variety of reasons, most of the units he counted on adding to his army would not reach him during the upcoming campaign.

For a while the stealthy departure of the Army of Northern Virginia went without a hitch. On June 5 it seemed as if Hooker had suspected what Lee was doing when a small Federal force under Sedgwick stormed across the Rappahannock in the same area occupied the previous month. After carefully observing the Yankee soldiers do very little for forty-eight hours, Lee saw no reason to suspend his operation. He departed Fredericksburg that same day, reaching Culpeper June 7.

Ironically, it was a misreading of the signs by Hooker's intelligence unit that brought on the first major clash of the new campaign. Hooker caught wind of Stuart's cavalry gathering outside Culpeper and, believing it portended a raid behind Union lines, sent his cavalry to disrupt it. The result was the war's largest mounted engagement at Brandy Station on June 9. Lee's assessment afterward was that even though the fight had been a severe one, the enemy still did not recognize that more and more of the Rebel infantry were now filling roads taking them north, though it did impose a one-day delay on the operation's next major phase, the movement of Ewell's Corps north from Culpeper.

Robert E. Lee spent some of June 10 composing a long, thoughtful letter to Jefferson Davis. He provided no information regarding his troop movements, but instead took issue with Confederate politicians and newspaper editors who vented public scorn on various Northern peace movements. It was Lee's view that Southern armies were "growing weaker" from lack of fresh recruits, so anything that divided Northern opinion was a good thing. He urged Davis "to give all the encouragement we can . . . to the rising peace party of the North." Lee also sent a note of encouragement to his son Rooney, slightly wounded in the leg at Brandy Station. "I wish I could see you," he wrote, "but I cannot."[20]

The first obstacle in the way of the Confederate march north was a Federal outpost at Winchester. On June 13, pursuant to Lee's orders, Richard Ewell stalked the Union garrison. Sunday, June 14, and Monday, June 15, were decisive days in this campaign. Ewell successfully scattered Winchester's defenders before moving one of his divisions across the Potomac at Williamsport, Longstreet's Corps departed Culpeper to follow Ewell, more of Hill's Corps eased out of Fredericksburg, and Union general Hooker finally comprehended that the Rebel army was moving.

Lee, who rode north from Culpeper on June 17, closely monitored the situations for his increasingly far-flung units. On June 19 he scolded Ewell for not pushing all his divisions across the Potomac with sufficient alacrity. "I very much regret that you have not the benefit of your whole corps," he wrote Ewell, "for, with that north of the Potomac, should we be able to detain General Hooker's army from following you, you would be able to accomplish as much, unmolested, as the whole army could perform with General Hooker in its front."[21] Ewell got the message. However, a rise in the Potomac due to recent rains prevented him from shifting his entire command across the river for the next two days.

Lee continued to battle on two fronts; he communicated with quasi-independent units operating in West Virginia and western Maryland for diversionary actions to relieve some of the enemy buildup against him, and he nagged at Richmond to forward the troops he felt due him. Lee added a new wrinkle to a suggestion he had made earlier to Jefferson Davis to bring P. G. T. Beauregard and troops from various coastal commands to Richmond. Lee now thought that if Beauregard and even a token force could be established in Culpeper as a skeletal Fourth Corps, Federal authorities would have to counter the threat by diverting troops from chasing Lee. When he received this note, Jefferson Davis scratched his head and filed it away as impractical.

In a private conversation at this time with Major General Isaac R. Trimble, present at headquarters as a supernumerary, Lee suggested that his personal aspirations had not waned. "We have again out-maneuvered the enemy," he told Trimble, adding that the great lead he enjoyed over Hooker would force the Yankee general "to follow us by forced marches. I hope with these advantages to accomplish some signal result, and to end the war if Providence favors us."[22]

Between June 16 and 21, Federal cavalry tried to penetrate the screen Jeb Stuart had established in the Loudoun Valley, east of the Blue Ridge Mountains. There were sharp fights at Aldie (June 16), Middleburg (June 19), and Upperville (June 21), but the screen held, though portions of Longstreet's command were drawn east through the gaps as support. This delayed Longstreet, thus allowing Hill's Corps to take the middle position in the long infantry column tramping inexorably into Pennsylvania.

On June 22, with Ewell's Corps now north of the Potomac, Lee gave its commander his mission parameters. Ewell was to maintain his advance into Pennsylvania, fanning out eastward in three separate columns, maximizing the area he could scour for supplies, his objective being the Susquehanna River. Lee provided Ewell a very wide discretion. "If Harrisburg comes within your means, capture it," he said. Of course, everything depended on what Lee termed the "development of circumstances."[23]

Up to this point Stuart's cavalry had done a fine job protecting the right flank of Lee's marching columns from Yankee probing. However, because of this, the cavalrymen were held in stasis while the infantry columns marched northward, leaving Stuart well behind Ewell's vanguard. Lee needed Stuart's eyes at the head of his lengthening column, so his cavalry chief's problem became how to get there. He could try to push his men forward using roads already clogged with files of marching infantry and slow wagon trains. Or he could cut loose from the main columns to dash around the Yankee army and connect with Ewell in Pennsylvania.

Lee gave Stuart the green light for the more risky option on June 21 with the understanding that Stuart's overriding priority was to link with Ewell's advance. Stuart departed early on the morning of June 25 with three brigades, leaving behind a pair to service Lee's needs. The officers commanding these two brigades were not known to the general, nor did they enjoy the easy access Stuart had to army headquarters. Consequently, Lee would seriously underutilize these valuable mounted units in the critical days ahead.

Lee himself crossed the Potomac on June 25. As his party reached the Maryland side it was met, recollected an artilleryman present, by "several patriotic ladies with small feet and big umbrellas" who insisted on presenting Lee with a large wreath.[24] A round of delicate negotiation ended when a courier took the bulky offering with the general's thanks. All around them, recalled one of Longstreet's officers, "the inspiriting strains of 'Dixie' burst forth from bands of music."[25] Lee had just finished one dispatch to Richmond covering now familiar themes and would send a second before the day was over. These would be Lee's last messages to Davis until July 4. As he explained: "I have not sufficient troops to maintain my communications, and therefore have to abandon them."[26]

He was taking huge risks now. With Ewell's Corps well in the advance (portions of it passed through Gettysburg on June 26), followed by A. P. Hill followed by Longstreet, his army was too stretched out to fight. Lee counted on knowing where and when the enemy was concentrating early enough to gather his forces in time. Having an active and effective cavalry force at his beck and call was critical. He was now operating in unfriendly territory where he could not count on sympathetic civilians to provide him with useful directions or intelligence.

On June 27, Lee issued his General Order No. 73 from Chambersburg, Pennsylvania. The document praised the "high spirit" and "fortitude" his men had shown, but then took them to task for "instances of forgetfulness" involving the "destruction of private property." It concluded with a firm entreaty for his men "to abstain with most scrupulous care from unnecessary or wanton injury to private property," and it enjoined his officers to inflict "summary punishment" on violators.[27]

While Lee's directive prohibited personal and wanton acts, it allowed for whole categories of confiscation. Horses, cattle, sheep, and all kinds of foodstuffs were fair game. Also fair game were African Americans caught in the path of the Confederate advance. Although no formal orders were ever issued directing a round-up of Pennsylvania's black civilians, such actions took place with an openness and on a scale that suggests, at the very least, tacit knowledge at the highest levels. While exact numbers are not known, certainly more than a hundred African Americans (some escaped slaves but most freeborn) were herded South to be put into slavery.

Lee expected Stuart to reconnect by June 28. With no word that day, he ordered scouts to try to locate his wayward cavalry chief. In his increasing anxiety, Lee seemed to have forgotten about the two brigades Stuart had left behind. Not for another day would those units begin to move from the rear of Lee's long column toward the head.

Robert E. Lee's progression into Pennsylvania followed a prudent pattern. As he explained to Jefferson Davis on June 2, "if I am able to move, I propose to do so cautiously, watching the result."[28] For the previous few days he had allowed Ewell's Corps to push toward Harrisburg while keeping Hill and Longstreet at Chambersburg as he gauged the Federal reaction. The relative ease with which Ewell had carried out his instructions convinced Lee that the time was right to take the next step. Orders were prepared for Longstreet and Hill to resume the advance on June 29; the former to support Ewell, the latter to push east as far as the Susquehanna River.

Lee again spoke with General Trimble, who never forgot what was said. The enemy army, Lee predicted, "will come up, probably through Frederick; broken down with hunger and hard marching, strung out on a long line and much demoralized, when they come into Pennsylvania. I shall throw an overwhelming force on their advance, crush it, follow up the success, drive one corps back and another, and by successive repulses and surprises before they can concentrate; create a panic and virtually destroy the army."[29]

Lee's plans did not survive twenty-four hours. That night, at about 10:00 P.M., he learned from one of Longstreet's irregular but trustworthy scouts that the Union army was across the Potomac and concentrating around Frederick, much closer than he had

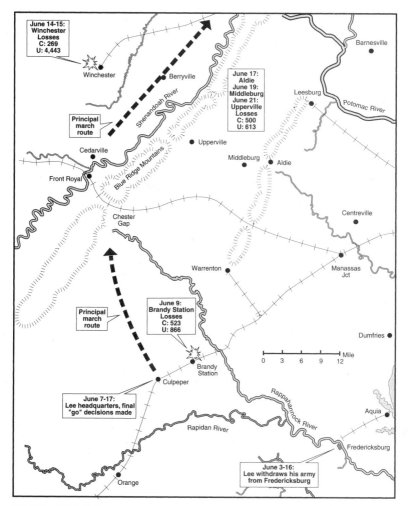

June 14-15:
Winchester
Losses
C: 269
U: 4,443

Winchester

Berryville

June 17:
Aldie
June 19:
Middleburg
June 21:
Upperville
Losses
C: 500
U: 613

Leesburg

Barnesville

Potomac River

Shenandoah River

Principal
march
route

Cedarville

Upperville

Middleburg

Aldie

Front Royal

Blue Ridge Mountains

Centreville

Chester
Gap

Warrenton

Manassas
Jct

Principal
march
route

June 9:
Brandy Station
Losses
C: 523
U: 866

Dumfries

0   3   6   9   12

Mile

Brandy
Station

Culpeper

Rappahannock River

Aquia

June 7-17:
Lee headquarters, final
"go" decisions made

Rapidan River

Fredericksburg

June 3-16:
Lee withdraws his army
from Fredericksburg

Orange

THE GETTYSBURG CAMPAIGN (1)

imagined possible at that date. The imminent danger was that the enemy columns would utilize the fine road system to march west through the mountains and into the Shenandoah Valley, bringing them up behind Lee. If true, he risked being caught at a disadvantage, with fully one-third of his army (Ewell's Corps) scattered off to the east. Lee needed to accomplish two objectives right away: stop the enemy from heading west, and bring his own army together.

New instructions were drawn up. Ewell was to pull back and concentrate near Cashtown on the eastern side of the South Mountain chain, while Hill's Corps was to march east through the mountains and attract attention to itself, hopefully causing the enemy to steer north from Frederick, rather than west. Lee disliked making these kind of alterations to his program based on a sole source report, but he felt he had no choice. Jeb Stuart's absence loomed increasingly large in his thinking.

His concerns bubbled to the surface on June 29. This morning Lee had occasion to speak with an officer on Ewell's staff who was passing through Chambersburg on his way to rejoin his command. At one point in their discussion, Lee asked if he had heard anything of Jeb Stuart. The young captain recalled meeting a pair of cavalrymen who reported that Stuart was still in Virginia on June 28. "The General was evidently surprised and disturbed," the officer later wrote. Lee waved over one of his staff officers, Walter Taylor, and had the story repeated. A few moments later, standing alone with Taylor, the captain asked about Lee's obvious concern. Taylor replied that "General Lee expected General Stuart to report before that time in Pennsylvania, and that he was much disturbed by his absence, having no means of information about the movements of the enemy's forces."[30]

This appears to be the day that Lee learned that Joseph Hooker was gone and George Meade now commanded the Army of the Potomac. When someone asked Lee what he thought the change

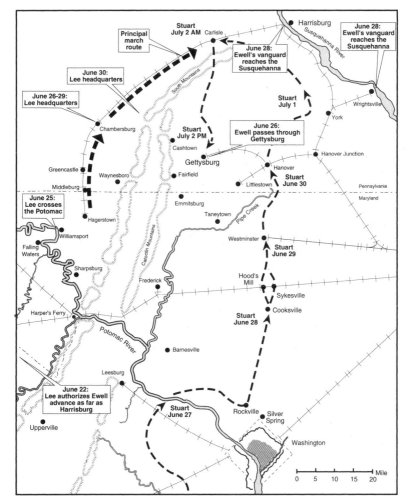

THE GETTYSBURG CAMPAIGN (2)

meant, he responded, "General Meade will commit no blunder in my front, and if I make one he will make haste to take advantage of it."[31] He displayed some more of his thinking on that June 29 when he greeted John B. Hood of Longstreet's Corps: "Ah, General, the enemy is a long time finding us; if he does not succeed soon, we must go in search of him."[32]

In his direction of the operation to this point, Lee had remained firmly focused on his ultimate objective. On the plus side this kept him from being distracted by the little cavalry war that had taken place at Brandy Station and in the Loudoun Valley during his march north. The absence of any serious effort by the Federal army to halt his operation convinced Lee that his analysis of the enemy's poor condition was correct. This bred an overconfidence that now clouded his judgment. When Stuart's cavalry, his best means to maintain a close watch on the enemy, temporarily went missing, Lee had no alternate plan to cover the intelligence loss. He then let too much time pass before reacting to Stuart's continued absence, and by then it was almost too late.

Robert E. Lee moved his headquarters on June 30 from a pleasant grove outside Chambersburg to the village of Greenwood at the western entrance to the Cashtown Gap. He gauged the enemy was a long day's march away at best and that the concentration he had ordered was taking place in an orderly fashion. When his army was whole again, Lee would number more than 70,000 fighting men in the ranks, most of them combat-wise and hungry for victory. He was confident he had sufficient time to prepare his army for the battle he hoped would decide the war.

CHAPTER 11

Gettysburg

It was Lee's intention to begin concentrating his army on the eastern side of the South Mountain chain and there await the enemy's approach. With A. P. Hill mostly through the Cashtown Pass and Ewell due to concentrate near him at Cashtown, this left only Longstreet's Corps, who marched the morning of July 1. A soldier who saw Lee as he accompanied the column thought the general "was looking in perfect health & seemed happy as the troops cheered him."[1]

As Longstreet's files converged on the western pass entrance they ran into a traffic snarl. One of Ewell's divisions had taken a more roundabout route than the other two and was now trying to march from west to east through the gap to join its parent unit. Lee decided that it was more important for Ewell to effect his concentration than to interpose the First Corps, so he instructed

Longstreet to delay until the Second Corps infantry and wagons cleared the way. For a while the officers stood dismounted, watching the soldiers shuffle past before continuing eastward.

The group slowly eased by the infantry ascending the western slope of the pass. As remembered by one of Lee's staff officers, they were approaching the crest when "firing was heard from the direction of Gettysburg. This caused Lee some little uneasiness. . . . [But he was] persuaded that the firing indicated a cavalry affair of minor importance."[2] Lee continued without increasing his pace toward Cashtown, where he expected to find A. P. Hill and learn exactly what was happening.

He reached the village about 11:00 A.M. Said one of the officers with him, "the sound [of firing in the direction of Gettysburg] had become heavy and continuous, and indicated a severe engagement."[3] Lee questioned A. P. Hill, who had no idea what all the firing was about, except that one of his three divisions (that was commanded by Major General Henry Heth) was supposed to be investigating reports of Federal horsemen in the town of Gettysburg. Hill headed to the town to find out about Heth, while Lee slowly followed.

Hardly had he departed when Lee learned that R. H. Anderson's Division of Hill's Corps was nearby, so he summoned the officer hoping that he might know what was happening. Anderson was as much in the dark as Lee. He then became the audience for a monologue from his army commander. "I cannot think what has become of Stuart," Lee said ("more to himself than me," Anderson noted). "In the absence of reports from him, I am in ignorance as to what we have in front of us here. It may be the whole Federal army, or it may be only a detachment. If it is the whole Federal force, we must fight a battle here."[4]

Not long after this incident, Lee rode toward Gettysburg along the Chambersburg (or Cashtown) Pike. The regular rumble of artillery fire was disturbing evidence that portions of his army were in

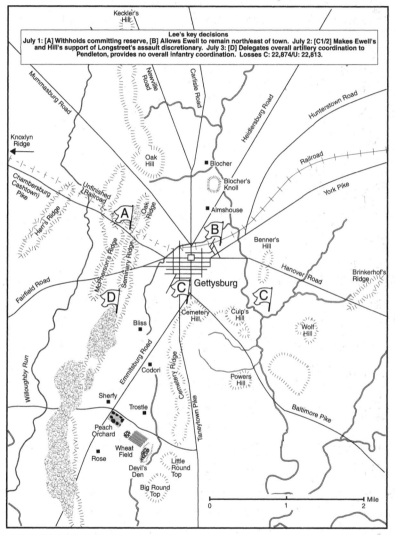

Lee's key decisions

July 1: [A] Withholds committing reserve, [B] Allows Ewell to remain north/east of town. July 2: [C1/2] Makes Ewell's and Hill's support of Longstreet's assault discretionary. July 3: [D] Delegates overall artillery coordination to Pendleton, provides no overall infantry coordination. Losses C: 22,874/U: 22,813.

Keckler's Hill
Mummasburg Road
Newville Road
Carlisle Road
Heidlersburg Road
Hunterstown Road
Knoxlyn Ridge
Oak Hill
Blocher
Blocher's Knoll
Railroad
Chambersburg (Cashtown) Pike
Unfinished Railroad
Herr's Ridge
Oak Ridge
Almshouse
York Pike
A
B
McPherson's Ridge
Seminary Ridge
Benner's Hill
Fairfield Road
Hanover Road
Brinkerhof's Ridge
D
C Gettysburg
C
Bliss
Cemetery Hill
Culp's Hill
Wolf Hill
Willoughby Run
Emmitsburg Road
Codori
Cemetery Ridge
Powers Hill
Sherfy
Trostle
Peach Orchard
Wheat Field
Rose
Devil's Den
Little Round Top
Big Round Top
Taneytown Pike
Baltimore Pike

0   1   2   Mile

GETTYSBURG

serious combat. He was met approaching the town's outskirts by Campbell Brown, an aide to Richard Ewell, who informed him of a decision Ewell had made to alter orders by following a more direct route to Cashtown through Gettysburg instead of a longer one bypassing the town. Much to Brown's surprise, Lee immediately wanted to know if Ewell had heard anything from Jeb Stuart. When Brown answered in the negative, Lee seemed both anxious and angry. He ordered Ewell to make every effort to open communications with General Stuart, then dismissed the officer.

Lee crossed Knoxlyn Ridge (still showing the debris of a morning skirmish) and halted atop a slight rise just west of Herr's Ridge and north of the pike. There he encountered A. P. Hill, whose situation report still lacked details. They were soon joined by Henry Heth, whose troops had been roughly handled in a morning's engagement along McPherson's Ridge that had gotten out of hand. Lee heard a confused tale of a small scrap against cavalry that had suddenly escalated into a full-blown battle when the Yankee horsemen had been reinforced by veteran infantry. Heth managed to stabilize a line along Herr's Ridge, just west of Gettysburg. Hardly had matters quieted down before Ewell's leading division under Major General Robert Rodes made its appearance from the north along the Newville Road and immediately closed with the enemy.

This was not supposed to happen. Ewell's orders were to not become heavily engaged until the army had concentrated. Lee was still digesting this turn of events when Henry Heth made an appearance.

"Rodes is very heavily engaged, had I not better attack?" he asked.

"No," Lee replied, "I am not prepared to bring on a general engagement to-day—Longstreet is not up."[5]

It was not long after this that Lee encountered Andrew R. Venable, a member of Jeb Stuart's staff finally come to report. Little of what he had to say was helpful. Stuart's cavalry was at least thirty miles distant and, when last seen, moving away from Gettysburg in what Lee knew would be a wasted effort to locate Ewell near Carlisle, Pennsylvania. No account of Venable's conversation with Lee was preserved. The cold reality was that he could expect no help soon from Jeb Stuart.

Lee had not anticipated today's fight. Even when he found one of his divisions embroiled in a serious little engagement he had kept the lid on the action lest it expand into a major affair. Hardly had he reined in Hill and Heth before Ewell's men restoked the conflict. Now Ewell had his hands full. Thanks to Heth's inactivity, imposed by Lee, the Federals were shifting units from McPherson's Ridge to meet the northern threat. The situation had slipped from Lee's grasp. He was no long the master of events but was instead being controlled by them.

Henry Heth came back to report what the Federals were doing and again sought permission to attack. Lee's reply, as remembered by Heth, was: "Wait a while and I will send you word when to go in."[6] Lee had decided. There would be more fighting today at Gettysburg. Under his orders, Confederate forces west of Gettysburg joined with those coming down from the north in an all-out effort.

North of the city, Rodes's and Early's divisions of Ewell's Corps battered the unlucky Union Eleventh Corps, flanked it off Blocher's Knoll, and herded it through Gettysburg. To the east, a pair of Heth's divisions drove forward in the face of stubborn Union defensive stands along McPherson's and Seminary ridges, sending the enemy streaming back through Gettysburg's increasingly chaotic streets. Jubilant Rebels crowded into town.

Robert E. Lee rode toward Gettysburg amid his victorious soldiers. A field headquarters was established near Seminary Ridge even as the last Federal defenders fell back to Cemetery Hill, just south of the town. A. P. Hill was feeling cocky. He believed that the Yankees had been completely routed, while Lee's own observation revealed that many of the Federal units were maintaining cohesion as they retreated.

He had unwillingly been drawn into the fray only when it seemed that the advantage secured by Ewell's timely arrival would be squandered if the enemy were allowed to combine against him. Hill's Corps had suffered greatly claiming its victories, so much so that Lee felt that these two divisions had reached their limit. But the job was not finished. Observing that the Federals were reorganizing on Cemetery Hill, he called on his staff officer Walter Taylor, directing him "to go to General Ewell and to say to him that, from the position which he occupied, he could see the enemy retreating over those hills . . . , that it was only necessary to press 'those people' in order to secure possession of the heights, and that, if possible, he wished him to do this."[7]

Taylor departed. Not quite three miles west of Lee's position were 7,000 more of Hill's men, veterans for the most part, not yet engaged this day. Major General Richard H. Anderson had marched his division from Cashtown, reaching Knoxlyn Ridge just after 4:00 P.M. According to his later recollection, he was met by a messenger from General Lee with instructions for him to halt and bivouac his division. After issuing the necessary orders to his subordinates, a perplexed Anderson rode forward to confirm it, reaching Lee not long after Walter Taylor had departed. Lee informed Anderson that there was no error, "that he was in ignorance as to the force of the enemy in front, . . . and that a reserve in case of disaster, was necessary."[8]

James Longstreet showed up at Lee's headquarters a little after 5:00 P.M. Lee was busy when Longstreet arrived, so the First Corps commander used the opportunity to review conditions, especially Cemetery Hill, a point that still concerned Lee. Lee summoned staff officer Colonel Armistead Long and, as the man remembered, "directed me to reconnoiter the position to which the enemy had retired."[9]

Longstreet thought a frontal assault on entrenched high ground was a bad idea, so when Lee joined him he immediately suggested they disengage in order to seek the enemy's southern (or left) flank. Lee was surprised at Longstreet's proposal, especially as the First Corps commander had no understanding of the overall situation. "If the enemy is there tomorrow," Lee answered, pointing toward Cemetery Hill, "we must attack him." All of Longstreet's concerns about the current campaign welled up in a rare burst of insubordinate testiness. "If he is there, it will be because he is anxious that we should attack him," Longstreet said, "a good reason, in my judgment for not doing so." Thinking back upon this moment, Longstreet believed that "General Lee was impressed with the idea that, by attacking the Federals [on Cemetery Hill], he could whip them in detail."[10]

A third figure joined the group. It was Captain James Power Smith, aide to Richard Ewell. He informed Lee that Ewell was prepared to assault some heights south of the town (East Cemetery Hill) if he could be assured of a cooperative attack against the high ground on his right flank (Cemetery Hill). Lee passed the young officer his binoculars, pointing as he did so to Cemetery Hill, saying that he supposed it was the high ground that Ewell meant. Lee informed Smith that "he had no force on the field with which to take that position," and asked Longstreet how near his closest division was. Longstreet thought six miles, but volunteered little else regarding its availability. Lee repeated his wish that Ewell "take the [East] Cemetery Hill if it were possible."[11] Smith departed with this message.

Longstreet understood Lee's reaction as conditionally rejecting his idea. "The sharp battle fought by Hill and Ewell on that day had given him a taste of victory," he commented afterward. "I believed that he had made up his mind to attack," Longstreet declared. Still, when he returned to his troops sometime after 5:30 P.M. he was confident that Lee "had not yet determined as to when the attack should be made."[12]

Despite his statements, Lee was not completely convinced that he should maintain the offensive at Gettysburg, but it would require more than Longstreet's worries to change his mind. Staff officer Long rejoined the general to report that Cemetery Hill was "occupied by a considerable force, . . . and . . . an attack at that time . . . would have been hazardous."[13] Then aide Walter Taylor returned from visiting Ewell, certain that the Second Corps commander would try to carry the East Cemetery heights before ending this day's fight. Lee realized that much was riding on a situation about which he knew very little, so he decided to speak directly with Ewell.

He met him at the Second Corps headquarters, located in a small house near the Carlisle Road. It was their first face-to-face meeting since June 9. Ewell's standing orders had been to avoid a general engagement, but much to his relief his superior had not come to chew him out for ignoring the directive. Lee wanted to know just two things: the condition of the Second Corps and its ability to renew the attack in the morning. Present were two of Ewell's division commanders, generals Robert Rodes and Jubal Early; the third, Edward Johnson, was quite busy getting his division into position near some high ground further east known as Culp's Hill. While both of Ewell's subordinates were positive about their combat readiness to fight, neither felt that the ground there was suitable for significant offensive operations.

Lee was serious about attacking on July 2 and pressed Ewell for options. Was the area assigned to Johnson's Division a possibility? he asked. Early indicated it was not. In addition to what he had observed this day, Early had surveyed the area when he passed through on June 26. He was certain that the terrain was too rugged and steep, and since the town's narrow streets made it difficult to stage troops for an assault, they would have to deploy in open fields, well within enemy cannon range. Even if they were successful, Early concluded, it would "be at a very great loss."[14]

Early pointed to the south, along Cemetery Ridge, where more high ground was visible. Take control of that, he argued, and the enemy would have to abandon Cemetery Hill. Ewell and Robert Rodes firmly seconded this opinion, effectively making it someone else's problem. Ewell seemed content to let the Second Corps rest on its laurels.

"Then perhaps I had better draw you around toward my right, as the line will be very long and thin if you remain here, and the enemy may come down and break through it," Lee wondered.[15] Again Early disagreed. To pull his men back now, he stated, after they had fought so hard to take the town would be a blow to their morale. There was also the question of the wounded who could not be removed quickly enough. Ewell and Rodes once more backed Early.

It never occurred to Lee to just issue peremptory orders for Ewell to attack or to withdraw. The prospect of imposing his will on a subordinate was simply too foreign to his nature. Yet the situation demanded action on July 2. The two divisions of Hill's Corps had taken heavy casualties this day and were in no condition to renew the attack. Ewell and his division commanders had firmly opted themselves out of any principal continuing role. That left Longstreet, who had already crossed a tacit line of respectful behavior with his nearly insubordinate outburst. Carrying a collection of poor options, Lee returned to his headquarters.

The more he mulled over matters on his return ride, the less sense it made to keep Ewell's Corps swung around where it was. Shortly after reaching Seminary Ridge he sent staff officer Charles Marshall over to Ewell with orders for the Second Corps to sidle around to the south. When Marshall completed his trek, just after 10:30 P.M., Ewell was with him. Things had changed, the Second Corps commander explained. Johnson's brigades had moved up and if they hadn't already taken control of Culp's Hill, they would be doing so very soon. That would put them in a wonderful position to interdict Federal supplies rolling along the Baltimore Pike, as well as providing a good platform for assaulting Cemetery Hill. It would be wrongheaded to relinquish it, Ewell argued.

Lee was skeptical that the Federals would leave something so critical to their defense unprotected, but such oversights in the heat of battle were not unknown. The formerly hesitant and reserved Ewell now seemed so certain that Lee reversed himself. The Second Corps would hold its place. He would find a part for it to play on July 2.

Regarding his overall objective, Lee had not changed his mind at all. A battle had been started today, but not finished. He would complete it tomorrow. All the strategic reasons he had discussed so long ago with Jefferson Davis compelled him to engage the enemy's main army during this campaign. Chance had made the place Gettysburg. There was another reason to press on, as well. The Federals had fought well and they could not be allowed time to draw pride from that experience. As he later recorded: "Encouraged by the successful issue of the engagement of the first day, and in view of the valuable results that would ensue from the defeat of the army of General Meade, it was thought advisable to renew the attack."[16]

Sunrise, July 2, came at 4:37 A.M., but Robert E. Lee was moving about well before then. With his late sessions with Richard Ewell and the duties of his position, he had snatched perhaps two or three hours of rest that night. Right after a hasty breakfast he was striding off toward the Lutheran Seminary, where he could examine the western face of Cemetery Hill as well as monitor activity as far east as Benner's Hill and south toward the Coderi farm. Lee had half expected the Federals to be gone, but not only was the Union army still on the high ground, it was also obvious that reinforcements had reached it during the night. Enemy units now occupied a line that stretched southward from Cemetery Hill along Cemetery Ridge.

James Longstreet joined Lee before sunrise. The First Corps commander had also breakfasted early before heading to Lee's headquarters with a retinue including several of the foreign officers accompanying the army, Englishman Arthur Fremantle among them. While Longstreet advanced alone to confer with Lee, Fremantle climbed a nearby tree with another observer, Justus Scheibert. The Prussian major, who had been with this army at Chancellorsville, offered the opinion that Lee was "not at his ease," and appeared "care-worn."[17]

About this time Lee heard from Ewell that when Edward Johnson's troops advanced to occupy Culp's Hill earlier that morning they found it full of Federals. The principal reason he had allowed Ewell's Corps to remain awkwardly wrapped around Gettysburg's northside was no longer valid, but it was too late to change.

Longstreet immediately picked up where he had left off by expressing his opinion that assaulting the high ground was a poor option. Lee remained committed to attack, but where to strike was the question. He needed eyes closer to the enemy and so called forward a captain of engineers on his staff named Samuel R. Johnston. "General Lee . . . said he wanted me to reconnoiter along the enemy's left and return as soon as possible," remembered the officer.[18]

Lee was also pondering how he could best use the Second Corps, representing his army's left. Staff officer Charles Venable was dispatched to corps headquarters with orders to reconnoiter the ground in front of those troops and determine if an attack might be mounted against Cemetery Hill despite yesterday's comments by Early and others.

A. P. Hill came over from his headquarters, accompanied by Henry Heth. Up in his tree, Fremantle observed that Heth had received a slight head wound toward the end of yesterday's fighting. Francis Lawley, a British correspondent for the *London Times,* eyed Lee from a respectful distance. The reporter thought the Rebel chieftain appeared "more anxious and ruffled than I had ever seen him before, though it required close observation to detect it."[19]

With daylight came the pop-pop-popping of skirmishing. Needing to hear from the various officers he had dispatched, Lee stayed on a short leash. The Prussian observer Scheibert recalled him "riding to and fro, frequently changing his position, making anxious inquiries here and there."[20] Likely at this time Richard Ewell, suspecting that Lee would wonder about the firing on his front, sent his aide Campbell Brown to report and request instructions.

As the aide remembered it, Lee instructed him "to tell Gen[era]l E[well] to be sure not to become so much involved as to be unable readily to extricate his troops, 'for I have not decided to fight here, and may probably draw off by my right flank . . . , so as to get between the enemy & Washington & Baltimore, & force them to attack us in position.'"[21]

Samuel R. Johnston returned from his scout of the Federal left flank around 8:00 A.M. He came bearing important news. His party of four had followed a route offering plenty of concealment that enabled them to cross the Emmitsburg Road near a peach orchard. Passing over an open field, the group partially ascended one of a pair of dark hills, giving the officer an impressive view of the surrounding area, which appeared empty of Union soldiers. Descending the hill, the party moved south, then west, looping back toward Lee's headquarters. Along the way they dodged a Federal cavalry patrol prowling the Emmitsburg Road.

"General Lee saw me and called me to him," the young officer recollected. "I stood behind General Lee and traced on the map the route over which I had made the reconnaissance." When he came to the two eminences marking the climax of his journey, Johnston pointed to the smaller one, Little Round Top. He mentioned his partway climb up the slope and the fact that he had seen no Yankee troops save those on the road. Lee, recollected Johnston, "was surprised at my getting so far, but showed clearly that I had given him valuable information." Lee needed to be sure. "Did you get there?" he pressed Johnston, indicating Little Round Top on the map. "I assured him I did," Johnston replied.[22]

Johnston's report provided a critical piece for the plan that Lee was constructing based on a picture of the Federal position compounded from his own observations and scouting reports. Both were significantly flawed. Many historians doubt that Johnston could have gone where he said he went, since an entire Union corps had arrived during the night and camped in the very area he claimed to have visited. Lee's own observations left him with the impression that the enemy's main line of resistance tracked with the Emmitsburg Road when, in fact, it followed Cemetery Ridge, which diverged toward the east.

His resolve was unshaken. "The enemy is here, and if we do not whip him, he will whip us," he said to Brigadier General John B. Hood of Longstreet's Corps.[23] There seemed no possibility of a serious attack from the rugged Confederate left, and the enemy's strong position on Cemetery Hill ruled out an effort from A. P. Hill's sector. Lee had been hoping to find an opening on the Rebel right, and the mounting evidence suggested to him that there was one.

He asked Johnston to remain for another assignment. Longstreet's Corps would soon be marching to the area Johnston had scouted and he wanted the officer to help guide the columns. At some earlier point, Longstreet indicated to Lee that he preferred any attack be led by Major General Lafayette McLaws and his division. So when the thickly bearded commander appeared about 8:30 A.M., Lee was ready with instructions.

The imminent prospect of battle helped focus his mind. McLaws thought that the army commander "was as calm and cool as I ever saw him." Lee spread out a map of the vicinity, pointing as he did so to a line drawn perpendicularly to the Emmitsburg Road near Sherfy's peach orchard, where he believed the Federal position terminated. "General, I wish you to place your division across the road, and I wish you to get there if possible without being seen by the enemy." Lee looked hard at McLaws. "Can you get there?" he asked.

McLaws answered that he knew of no reason why he could not make the movement requested. Actually, he had nary a clue regarding the lay of the land, so when Lee mentioned Johnston's survey, McLaws, misunderstanding the context, asked to accompany that officer. Longstreet promptly intervened. "No, sir, I do not wish you to leave your division," he said, not bothering to explain that Johnston's reconnaissance had already occurred.

Even as McLaws was absorbing this, Longstreet ran his finger on the map and indicated an orientation at an acute angle to the one designated by Lee. "I wish your division placed so," Longstreet said.[24] Lee firmly corrected his First Corps commander before allowing McLaws to depart to prepare his division. Prior to leaving, McLaws once more asked permission to accompany Johnston and Longstreet once more refused the request.

There only remained finding a role for Ewell's Corps. Charles Venable had not yet reported back, so Lee decided to make another personal visit. It was approaching 9:00 A.M. when he departed for his Second Corps headquarters, but upon arriving he learned that its commander was reconnoitering his lines with Lee's aide. Major General Isaac Trimble, who happened to be present, said he knew just the place when Lee asked to be shown a good vantage point. Trimble led the way to the village almshouse, which boasted a cupola with a view. Lee could see that the Federals on Cemetery Hill were not hopelessly disorganized. According to Trimble, Lee told him: "The enemy have the advantage of us in a short and inside line, and we are too much extended."[25]

They returned to Ewell's headquarters to find the Second Corps leader still absent. Ewell finally arrived with Charles Venable in tow, who was now fully convinced that conditions on this flank would seriously hamper any offensive effort. His earnest seconding of Ewell's previous arguments confirmed Lee's conclusion the Second Corps might at best offer diversionary support for a main assault against the opposite flank.

After departing Ewell's headquarters, Lee returned to his own where he checked on Longstreet's preparations. Riding along Seminary Ridge, he passed through an artillery position that he thought belonged with Longstreet's column. The officer commanding tactfully indicated his guns reported to the Third Corps. Lee apologized, asking: "Do you know where General Longstreet is?" Colonel R. Lindsay Walker, A. P. Hill's artillery chief, offered himself as guide. "As we rode together," Walker later recalled, "General Lee manifested more impatience than I ever saw him exhibit upon any other occasion."[26]

Lee heard from Longstreet that all of McLaws's Division was on hand, ready to proceed, and Hood's Division lacked only McLaw's Alabama Brigade to be complete. Its arrival was expected any moment, so Longstreet asked permission to delay executing his orders until it showed. According to Longstreet's recollection, "General Lee assented. We waited about forty minutes for these troops."[27]

Lee later described the day's battle plan thus: "It was determined to make the principal attack upon the enemy's left, and endeavor to gain a position [in the peach orchard] from which it was thought that our artillery could be brought to bear with effect. Longstreet was directed to place the divisions of McLaws and Hood on the right of Hill, partially enveloping the enemy's left, which he was to drive in. General Hill was ordered to threaten the enemy's center, to prevent re-enforcements being drawn to either wing, and co-operate with his right division in Longstreet's attack. General Ewell was instructed to make a simultaneous demonstration upon the enemy's right, to be converted into a real attack should opportunity offer."[28]

The sun hadn't passed its noon position before the two available divisions of Longstreet's Corps (the third, Pickett's, was transiting the Cashtown Pass) commenced their flank march. Lee accompanied Longstreet for a short distance. After departing the column, he returned to his morning's observation post. Watching him was the British observer, Fremantle, once again up in his tree after touring Gettysburg. A flare up of skirmishing around the Bliss farm, located in a no-man's land between the opposing lines, provided the background as Lee joined A. P. Hill, whose principal task this day was to make certain that each of his division commanders knew their part in the scheme of things as they represented the critical junction between Longstreet and Ewell. From the evidence of what transpired, this was something that Hill failed to do.

Jeb Stuart made a much belated appearance about this time, having finally completed his mission. Lee appears to have passed over Stuart's late arrival without comment, although some postwar memoirs manufactured a bit of dialogue to show his displeasure. Perhaps the imminent battle kept him from investing much personal capital in the moment. Stuart departed as quickly as he had arrived. In his official report, he wrote only that his new orders were to take position on the left wing of the Army of Northern Virginia. Lee saved his final judgment for his official report where he noted that the army's movements leading up to the battle "had been much embarrassed by the absence of cavalry."[29]

Stuart's visit was so brief and uneventful that the English observer Fremantle missed him entirely and would not actually meet the cavalry chief for several days. Fremantle remembered watching Lee maintain his position "nearly all the time; looking through his field-glass—sometimes talking to Hill and sometimes to Colonel Long [street] of his Staff. But generally he sat quite alone on the stump of a tree."[30]

There is evidence that Lee had an emergency conversation with James Longstreet. Another foreign military observer, Englishman

FitzGerald Ross, recalled the two having a long consultation. The Federal left flank was not arrayed as Lee had expected it to be, and Longstreet needed some wiggle room in his attack orders. Apparently he got it. At long last, at about 3:40 P.M., the throaty rumble of massed cannon firing to the south signaled that Longstreet's assault was beginning.

Then began the rattle of musketry, the individual shots blurring into a sound often likened to the tearing of sheets. For perhaps fifty minutes this cacophony seemed locked in place, as if the combat had stalled in one area. Not until roughly 6:30 P.M. did it begin to roll closer and closer to where Lee waited. By 7:15 P.M. the fighting spread to a point under Lee's direct observation as troops belonging to Hill's Corps picked up the advance and moved toward the Emmitsburg Road. Then, inexplicably, it began to sputter out as the untidy remnants of regiments and even brigades could be seen drifting back toward their jump-off points.

According to Arthur Fremantle, during the hours of combat along the Emmitsburg Road, Lee "only sent one message, and only received one report."[31] An artilleryman posted nearby observed that throughout the late afternoon Lee's "countenance betrayed no more anxiety than upon the occasion of a general review."[32]

It was not quite 10:00 P.M. when serious firing erupted toward East Cemetery and Culp's hills on Ewell's front. This provoked sudden activity along the Federal lines as soldiers rushed toward the fresh outburst. Mixed in with the gunfire were the distinctive sounds of the high-pitched Rebel yell and the deeper throated Yankee huzzah. It wasn't until after 11:00 P.M. that the entire front settled into a moody silence. Lee likely returned to his headquarters along the Chambersburg Pike to sift through action reports.

From his way of thinking, all of the results were positive. It was true that at no point had his men achieved the kind of breakthrough he had sought, but nor had his troops ended the day empty-handed. "Longstreet succeeded in getting possession of and holding the desired ground," Lee later wrote, adding that "Ewell also carried some of the strong positions which he assailed."[33]

The desired ground Lee mentioned was around the Sherfy family's peach orchard which, he believed, swelled high enough to dominate the Yankee lines along Cemetery Ridge. Had Lee another chance to speak with Longstreet's able artillery chief, E. P. Alexander, he would have learned that the ground rose again some forty feet at the Federal main line of resistance, so packing the peach orchard with his cannon provided none of the advantages he imagined it did. Similarly, Ewell's report suggested he had penetrated the enemy's principal defensive lines when, in fact, his troops had taken possession of trenches abandoned by the Federals located well down the slope from their strongly fortified hilltop. Yet it was upon this flawed data that Lee based his plans for July 3.

Of his three corps commanders only A. P. Hill reported in person to Lee this night. None of Lee's principal staff officers recorded any visits to the First or Second corps. Both Ewell and Longstreet sent others with their summaries, though it was unusual for his First Corps commander to absent himself. It was not uncommon for reports of the damage done to the enemy to be exaggerated, and even allowing for a little reasonable skepticism, Lee believed that the Union army had been heavily damaged. Apparently very little was conveyed to him regarding the condition of the Rebel units that had fought this day. While the names of prominent officers missing, killed, or known wounded were quickly known, details regarding the combat efficiency of those brigades were not. Having experienced the nearly miraculous recuperative powers his soldiers had demonstrated on past occasions, Lee assumed that they would be ready after a short rest to fight again. To his advantage, he could now count on Stuart's cavalry, plus there was a fresh infantry division at hand in the form of George E. Pickett's command. Having composed a picture of an enemy army on the ropes, and buoyed by his faith in his men, he determined to press ahead.

"The result of this day's operations induced the belief that with proper concert of action, and with the increased support that the positions gained on the right [by Longstreet] would enable the artillery to render the assaulting columns, we should ultimately succeed," Lee concluded, "and it was accordingly determined to continue the attack. The general plan was unchanged. Longstreet, re-enforced by Pickett's three brigades, . . . was ordered to attack the next morning, and General Ewell was directed to assail the enemy's right at the same time."[34]

Jeb Stuart would also have a part to play, though exactly what he was to do was not specified in any report. The only direct evidence comes from Stuart's adjutant general, Major Henry B. McClellan, who was in a position to know. According to the staff officer, "Stuart's object was to gain position where he would protect the left of Ewell's corps, and would also be able to observe the enemy rear and attack it in case the Confederate assault on the Federal lines were successful. He proposed, if opportunity offered, to make a diversion which might aid the Confederate infantry to carry the heights held by the Federal army."[35]

Another Rebel officer visiting Lee's headquarters late this night thought that the "commanding general looked well. He was all himself, and never appeared to better advantage." Lee emerged from his tent upon hearing the voice of A. P. Hill and made it a point to publicly shake his hand. "It is all well, General," Lee said, "everything is well."[36]

Robert E. Lee's orders to James Longstreet were to "attack the next morning" (July 3) according to the "general plan" of July 2.[37] The army commander offered no further specifics in any of his post-Gettysburg reports. When he checked with Longstreet to find out how far along his morning preparations were he was in for an unwelcome surprise. Longstreet greeted his chief: "General, I have had my scouts out all night, and I find that you still have an excellent opportunity to move around to the right of Meade's army and maneuver him into attacking us."

Lee diplomatically limited his post-battle comments regarding this moment to the terse statement that "General Longstreet's dispositions were not completed as early as was expected." Longstreet offered no apologies in his report, stating that his interpretation of the broad directives Lee granted him justified spending time investigating the possibilities for a flanking maneuver. Realizing that he had been unclear regarding his intention, Lee pointed with his fist toward Cemetery Ridge. "The enemy is there, and I am going to strike him," he said. He was not interested in any flank move. He still expected that the two First Corps divisions already on the field plus Pickett would renew the action.

Longstreet suddenly understood that the July 2 summary he sent Lee had neglected to make clear the battered state of those two divisions. He now laid out the facts as he knew them; "that the point had been fully tested the day before, by more men, when all were fresh; that the enemy was there looking for us . . . , [and that the enemy's units were well positioned to] strike the flank of the assaulting column, crush it, and get on our rear."

Lee listened to Longstreet's explanation, slowly comprehending that his attack scheme was resting on false premises. Yet he never considered suspending his offensive plans. "I am going to take them where they are on Cemetery Hill," he said, ending that part of the discussion.[38] Another way would have to be found to get at those people, and, as the steady reverberation of cannon and musketry fire that had been coming from Culp's Hill since dawn reminded him, found quickly.

The combat there had started at first light as Ewell tried again to overrun the fortress position the Federals had erected atop Culp's Hill. Hours earlier his men had failed to overcome a brigade's worth of troops holding it; during the night the position had been heavily reinforced and now Ewell's men faced many more of the enemy in a nearly impregnable position. Wave after wave of valiant men struggled up steep, rugged slopes in the face of continuous musketry that shredded bark and flesh. By the time Lee would be ready with his attack in the center, Ewell would have spent all his offensive energy in a lost cause. Incredibly, he seemed to have not understood that his effort was to be made in conjunction with Longstreet's, nor did Lee make any effort to restrain him.

While Lee and Longstreet began surveying the enemy lines to concoct a new attack plan, aides summoned A. P. Hill. The Third Corps commander joined the pair in front of Heth's Division. Although still woozy from his July 1 wounding, Henry Heth was also there as were several of Lee's staff, including Armistead Long, Walter Taylor and Charles Venable, the latter three keeping a respectful distance.

Lee wasn't yet ready to give up on utilizing McLaws's and Hood's divisions. Staff officer Taylor clearly "understood the argument to be that General Longstreet should endeavor to force the enemy's lines in his front. That front was held by the divisions of Hood and McLaws." By the time Armistead Long heard the conversation "it was decided that General Pickett should lead the assaulting column, to be supported by the divisions of McLaws and Hood and such other force as A. P. Hill could spare from his command." Longstreet renewed his objections to employing those shell-shocked units. "To have rushed forward my two divisions, then carrying bloody noses from their terrible conflict the day before, would have been madness," he commented later.

There was an awkward pause as Lee waited for one of his lieutenants to break the impasse. Then, A. P. Hill, whose performance on July 2 had been lackluster, suddenly spoke up, offering his entire corps for the effort. Lee thanked him and graciously noted the important central position his troops held, especially regarding the

Cashtown Pass. Still, the prospect of supplementing Pickett's fresh division with some of Hill's men was out in the open.

Someone, probably Henry Heth, volunteered his division for the task, an offer that Lee quickly accepted. Given his own shaky condition, it is unlikely that Heth was current on his command's combat readiness; perhaps there was still something he felt needed to be proven for the coarse way he had managed affairs on July 1. The selection of Heth's Division provided a focus point for the attack, since it was roughly opposite the Federal center. There was also space with concealment to the right of its line with room enough for Pickett's men.

With that, the main assault wave had been selected. Next was the matter of close support. Hill's efforts on July 2 had noticeably lacked in that regard, so he might have suggested it. Certainly only he could have recommended utilizing the two North Carolina brigades of Pender's Division to assist Heth. Pickett needed similar backup and here everyone must have turned to Longstreet who refused to consider using any part of McLaws's or Hood's divisions. It does not require much imagination to suspect that Hill appended two of Richard Anderson's brigades to attack roster.

Longstreet and Hill drew off to make preliminary arrangements. Longstreet had one more surprise waiting for him this morning when they returned to Lee, who indicated that his First Corps commander would direct the combined operation, even though Hill had committed as many if not more men. Speaking with a bluntness that perhaps he hoped would recuse him once and for all, Longstreet said: "General, I have been a soldier all my life. I have been with soldiers engaged in fights by couples, by squads, companies, regiments, divisions, and armies, and should know, as well as any one, what soldiers can do. It is my opinion that no fifteen thousand men ever arrayed for battle can take that position." Lee was unmoved. Still fresh in his mind was Hill's poor handling of troops on July 1 and July 2, so Longstreet got the assignment. "I said no more," reflected the First Corps commander.

According to Walter Taylor, "General Longstreet proceeded at once to make the dispositions for attack, and General Lee rode along the portion of the line held by A. P. Hill's Corps, and finally took position about the Confederate centre."[39] At some point around this time Lee briefed the army's artillery chief on what was expected of him. In his report, William N. Pendleton noted that at the "direction of the commanding general, the artillery along our entire line was to be prepared for opening . . . a concentrated and destructive fire, consequent upon which a general advance was to be made."[40]

Unable to remain inactive, Lee rode out toward Sherfy's peach orchard, soon encountering a skirmish line of Mississippi troops under Major George B. Gerald. The officer remembered Lee pointing "to the crest of a hill some two hundred yards distant and slightly to the rear and said he was going to place one hundred pieces of artillery there and for me to take a position so as to prevent the artillery from being harassed by federal infantry, which I did."[41]

His travels brought him to Pender's Division of Hill's Corps, which had fought hard and suffered much, including the loss of its commander, on July 1. Lee had tapped the unassigned officer, Major General Isaac Trimble, to take charge and now rode with him to review his troops. Trimble recalled that Lee seemed surprised at the number of men in the ranks who displayed bandages and other evidence of their hard times on July 1. "Many of these poor boys should go to the rear," Trimble remembered Lee's commenting. "They are not fit for duty." As they rode away from the lines of men, Trimble overheard Lee say, as if to himself, "the attack must succeed."[42]

Behind them, officers scrambled to work out operational elements of the plan. Two divisions, marching on a converging course, needed to be guided and regulated so that they came together at the right place and time. Units not already in their jump-off position had to be placed there. Artillery batteries were moved up and their commanders given their targets. What was known about the likely enemy resistance was communicated to the officers. The soldiers lucky (or unlucky) enough to glimpse the open ground they were to traverse returned to their comrades with somber faces.

Throughout the morning of planning and preparations, Lee never doubted he would succeed. As he later reported, "A careful examination was made of the ground secured [on July 2] by Longstreet, and his batteries placed in positions, which, it was believed, would enable them to silence those of the enemy. Hill's artillery and part of Ewell's was ordered to open simultaneously, and the assaulting column to advance under cover of the combined fire of the three. The batteries were directed to be pushed forward as the infantry progressed, protect their flanks, and support their attacks closely."[43]

His own examination of the ground, plus information gleaned from officers who had advanced across these fields on July 2, convinced Lee that his men would not suffer serious losses covering the distance from Seminary Ridge to the Emmitsburg Road. There were ripples and folds in the land that would shield his soldiers from the worst until they lost that cover crossing the Emmitsburg Road with something like a thousand feet to go. From that point forward Lee counted on the overpowering effect of his unprecedented artillery bombardment plus his aggressive deployment of mobile batteries with the advancing infantry to neutralize the enemy's advantages.

If the bombardment did its work, if the flanks were protected, and if enough of the artillery advanced with the infantry, Lee was certain that his superb soldiers would break the Yankee line. He counted on the Federal soldiers losing their nerve, and was utterly confident that his would press the attack all the way to Cemetery

Ridge. He had planned carefully, brought the best elements together, and made clear to all what he expected. It was all now in God's hands.

Lee was working at his headquarters when the guns opened. There had been no set time for the start of the Confederate bombardment, so he was as surprised as everyone else when it started a little after 1:00 P.M. Lee crossed the Chambersburg Pike and walked to a piece of high ground on the north side of the railroad cut, where he observed Captain William J. Reese's Jeff Davis (Alabama) Artillery in long-range action. According to a letter to a hometown Alabama newspaper, Lee praised the sweating gunners for "their unsurpassed chivalry."[44]

His movements after visiting the artillerymen are obscure. As he had on July 2, Lee left those entrusted with the responsibility freedom to operate. His continued reliance on Pendleton proved ill-founded. The army's artillery chief was decidedly ineffective in his efforts to coordinate fire from the Third and Second Corps batteries, leaving almost the entire burden on the 159 guns under Alexander. He also failed to position resupply munitions close enough to the front to be ready when requested. So when the time came for the batteries to advance with the infantry only a handful of individual guns could do so.

None of Lee's key staff, all of whom left postwar memoirs, carried any messages to the fighting troops. About the time the first wave was crossing the Emmitsburg Road, the British observer Fremantle, moving from Gettysburg along Seminary Ridge in search of Longstreet, noted "passing General Lee and his Staff." Fremantle made no further comment about the group, suggesting there was little happening. Right after leaving Lee, Fremantle did sight "many wounded men retiring from the front." He also encountered pieces of a Virginia brigade "flocking through the woods in numbers as great as the crowd in Oxford street in the middle of the day."[45] It is difficult to believe that Lee would not have noted this. The point would have been made when Lee met one of his brigadiers, J. Johnston Pettigrew, nursing a hand broken by a shell burst. With his aide alongside, Pettigrew was busy reforming his regiments as they stumbled back. It was while in the midst of this activity that he encountered Lee, who approved his actions. Before departing, Lee added: "General, I am sorry to see you wounded; go to the rear."[46]

Soon it was patently obvious that the grand assault had failed. (Afterward, Lee would learn that Stuart's effort off the far left Confederate flank had also been barren of results.) Men were streaming back from Cemetery Ridge in all combinations; some in ranks or fragments of ranks, others singly or in small groups. Lee's initial task was to see that his troops were rallied and his officers prepared to meet any contingency. The English observer Fremantle thought Lee's conduct at this time was "perfectly sublime. . . . His face . . . did not show signs of the slightest disappointment, care, or annoyance; and he was addressing to every soldier he met a few words of encouragement, such as, 'All this will come right in the end: we'll talk it over afterwards; but in the mean time, all good men must rally.'"

A wounded officer being helped to the rear recollected passing "General Lee, who was forming a line of the slightly wounded," while another in retreat found strength in Lee's composure, which he termed "ineffably grand."[47] Noting how intently Fremantle was watching him, Lee commented to the foreign observer: "This has been a sad day for us, Colonel—a sad day; but we can't expect always to gain victories."[48]

There were some personally painful moments for the general. When he encountered George Pickett and instructed him where to regroup his division, the grief-stricken officer itemized the fate of his brigadiers: "General Lee, I have no division now, [Lewis A.] Armistead is down, [Richard B.] Garnett is down, and [James L.] Kemper is mortally wounded." "Come, General Pickett," Lee replied, "this has been my fight and upon my shoulders rests the blame."[49] (Pickett's doleful summary was off in one regard; although badly wounded, Kemper survived the battle and the war.)

There is a persistent piece of the Gettysburg story that has Lee apologizing to his soldiers by telling them that the responsibility for their repulse was on his shoulders alone. When Lee's most distinguished biographer, Douglas Southall Freeman, came to write of these events, he titled his chapter: "It Is All My Fault." Lee's postwar partisans (Freeman among them) held that Lee did not make serious errors of command judgment, and that failures of his plans were due to the failings of others. By publicly taking the blame for his subordinates, Lee demonstrated qualities of charity and forgiveness that were central to the Christ-like image erected around him after his death. While this may have served a postwar agenda that sought to rewrite history, such a response from him must be docketed among Gettysburg's many myths. Lee had nothing to apologize for. He had fully performed his duty by crafting a plan with acceptable risks. Nothing in life was certain and while the events of this day were unfortunate, and it did truly pain him to see his men suffering, he had no cause for self-recrimination.

What was perhaps most important was that Lee abandoned any further plans for offensive action. All his decisions on July 2 and through the assault on July 3 minimized defensive planning to concentrate on an offensive objective. Now, however, it was time to think of saving the army. To insure no misunderstandings, Lee spoke with each of his corps commanders.

The first was James Longstreet, who recollected that it was decided to pull the First Corps back to the pre-assault positions it had held on July 2. Lee met with Richard Ewell around sunset. No longer would his corps hold its positions in and east of the town. The new line Lee was organizing ran roughly north to south along the axis of Seminary Ridge. Ewell's men would have the left flank. It was well after dark before Lee briefed A. P. Hill, whose corps essentially maintained its positions along lower Seminary Ridge. By inference, the two discussed a plan for Hill's men to lead the army's withdrawal from Gettysburg, set to begin in twenty-four hours unless the enemy attacked before then.

The heavy rain that had showered earlier in the evening scurried off as quickly as it had arrived, leaving the night sky scraped clean. The moon was high and the stars visible (although more clouds were building along the skirt of the horizon) as Brigadier General John D. Imboden waited near Lee's headquarters tent. The peacetime lawyer and businessman commanded a small unattached cavalry brigade that was then freelanced to headquarters. Imboden and his men had taken over watching the army's supply trains in Chambersburg from George Pickett's men before moving up to Gettysburg on the afternoon of July 3. The time was passing 11:00 P.M. when Imboden was told to report to Lee. Catching the army commander in conference with A. P. Hill, he waited at headquarters.

The cavalry officer guessed it was around 1:00 A.M. when Lee returned to his command post, weary beyond measure. He seemed to have trouble dismounting, and once he had gotten down he leaned against his horse and saddle, the picture of exhaustion.

"General, this has been a hard day on you," Imboden said, feeling he had to say something.

"Yes," Lee replied at last, "it has been a sad, sad day to us." The usually circumspect army commander followed another minute or so of silence with a brief soliloquy, alternately praising Pickett's men and bemoaning how his plan had not been implemented. With the anguish of a master designer who has seen one of his finest constructs fall victim to the failings of others, Lee allowed himself a rare venting. "Too bad! *Too bad!*" he exclaimed. "Oh! Too Bad!"[50]

Among his tasks, Imboden had to see that Lee's first report of the battle was delivered to Jefferson Davis. Necessarily brief, it also reflected some key elements as understood by Lee. At the end of July 1, the enemy "took up a strong position in rear of the town which he immediately began to fortify, and where his reinforcements joined him." The next day, July 2, Lee recounted his effort "to dislodge the enemy and though we gained some ground, we were unable to get possession of his position." Of his July 3 strike, Lee noted that the "works on the enemy's extreme right & left were taken, but his numbers were so great and his position commanding, that our troops were compelled to relinquish their advantage and retired." He closed the note with the comment that the Union army "suffered severely," adding a list of some of the important Confederate officers killed or wounded.[51] Since there was a real chance that this message might be intercepted, he offered no hint regarding his immediate plans.

Lee kept busy throughout July 4 preparing the army for its return to Virginia, but he made it a point to visit all parts of his line and to be seen by his men. The Texans cheered him as he passed their camps, a salute Lee acknowledged by raising his hat. He was spotted by several Union POWs, understandably interested in the mood of their enemy's leader. One thought Lee "showed no signs of worry. His countenance was placid and he appeared as cool and collected as if nothing unusual had transpired."[52]

Such times of great stress required even greater efforts at self-control. When an aide of Ewell's reported his command was prepared for action and somewhat smugly hoped the other two corps were as ready, Lee put the officer in his place. "What reason have you, young man, to suppose they are not?" he asked.[53] The object lesson aside, Lee did have enough doubts about the combat efficiency of Pickett's

Division that he assigned the shattered unit to the undesirable job of guarding Federal prisoners. While this decision was understandable under the circumstances, it was a slight that George Pickett never forgave or forgot.

Lee pulled up stakes toward nightfall to join Longstreet at his headquarters along the Fairfield Road. Once again it was raining hard off and on. The pair were encountered by the observer FitzGerald Ross, who noted they were "engaged in earnest conversation."[54] (Lee would later tell Ross that he was then considering halting the movement because of the atrocious weather, but that would have required turning the supply train around, something that was impossible.) Overheard by another in the group present, Lee admitted a personal failing. "I thought my men were invincible," he said.[55] Writing in what would be his second official Gettysburg report, Lee admitted that he may have asked more of his men "than they were able to perform."[56]

The withdrawal from Gettysburg, begun early on July 5, proved difficult in every way. While the great wagon train of the wounded struggled on muddy roads, following a route leading west through the Cashtown Pass then angling southward (avoiding Chambersburg) toward Williamsport, the infantry marched south along the eastern side of the mountains, passing through that barrier at Fairfield, following the shortest route to Hagerstown. The rains that so dogged their efforts and desperately slowed their progress also swelled the Potomac so that places where men had easily forded on their way into Pennsylvania were now impassable. A temporary pontoon bridge that Lee had maintained at Falling Waters had been destroyed by Yankee raiders on July 4. With no other alternative, on July 6 Lee began knitting his army into a defensive line stretching from just below Hagerstown to Falling Waters, its back to the flooded Potomac. His engineers turned in a magnificent job positioning the defenses and erecting earthworks at key points. Also magnificent was Jeb Stuart, whose cavalry effectively bought sufficient time for Lee's infantry to occupy this entrenched line.

Except for a few sharp attacks on his wagon train and several cavalry thrusts that only appeared threatening, Lee easily maintained his position through the night of July 13. Other than probing, Union general Meade did not give the Rebel army any serious challenge. Lee's men managed to erect emergency bridges and, beginning late on July 13, the bulk of the army successfully crossed to the Virginia side. The last two divisions to reach the bridge approaches were caught unprepared by a pair of Yankee cavalry divisions at Falling Waters, and before the confused fighting ended the Rebel fighters had lost some 700 as prisoners. Ironically, the parting shots of this campaign were fired from the command that opened the battle on July 1, Henry Heth's Division. This time, unlike after Sharpsburg, Lee did not seek a further confrontation with the Union army.

CHAPTER 12

To the End

On August 8, 1863, Robert E. Lee wrote a letter signaling the end of his military career. It was a note so explosive in its contents that he had set it down by hand, instead of relying on his headquarters staff to provide a first draft. Behind him now were the pressure-filled days following the battle of Gettysburg, when it seemed that God was determined to test him to the utmost. The time had come for blunt self-assessment, and no one was harder on Robert E. Lee than Lee himself.

"We must expect reverses, even defeats," he wrote in that letter to Jefferson Davis. "They are sent to teach us wisdom and prudence, to call forth greater energies, and to prevent our falling into greater disasters." Then he got to the point. "The general remedy for the want of success in a military commander is his removal . . . . I . . . propose to Your Excellency the propriety of selecting another commander for this army." Continuing in this vein, Lee cited the "growing failure of my bodily strength" and his belief "that a younger and abler man than myself can readily be attained."[1]

The reply from the Confederate President was not long in coming. Writing on August 11, Davis rejected Lee's request. "To ask me to substitute you by some one in my judgment more fit to command, or who would possess more of the confidence of the army, or of the reflecting men of the country, is to demand an impossibility," he declared.[2] The matter of Robert E. Lee's resignation was closed.

Still, the fact that Lee did attempt to resign merits some speculation. As someone not given to theatrical gestures, it is reasonable to assume that the impulse prompting the decision was real. Also, the absence of any negotiation involved in withdrawing it implies no greater a motive than a personal one. On paper at least, Lee's Pennsylvania raid accomplished all that he had advertised. He had supplied his army from the Union's bountiful larder, he had removed the destructive presence of Federal armies from the soil of northern Virginia, and he had made certain that his state's harvest season would proceed without interruption.

What Lee had failed to do—inflict a grievous defeat on the enemy's premier army—spoke to the core of his motivation. Based on what he said in his three Gettysburg reports, he believed that at the time of the battle his soldiers were fit and confident, and he had several clear opportunities to smash Meade's army. That he could not produce a decisive victory at that time said clearly that he would not be able to deliver such at any time. Lee was a soldier whose strategic vision and decision-making process needed a specific objective to give him the necessary focus. Gettysburg proved that the goal he had been pursuing was unattainable. Finding a new rationale to endure the physical and psychological hardships of active campaigning became a matter of personal importance in the weeks to come.

The next few months proved highly frustrating for the fifty-seven-year-old commander of the Confederacy's finest fighting army. He hardly had weathered the political fallout from his Gettysburg defeat when he was instructed to detach nearly a third of his army for service in a theater of the war far from Virginia. Lee argued to retain these men, but in this case Jefferson Davis decided that a crisis in the west had the greater priority. In early September 1863, James Longstreet's veteran infantry, along with its nearly indispensable commander, filed onto trains carrying them away from Virginia and into a battle that would be known as Chickamauga.

Just a few weeks later, Lee and his remaining soldiers were again in the field against their old foe, the Army of the Potomac. The operations in Culpeper, Fauquier, Prince William, and Orange counties in October and November resulted in no major engagements. It was more like shadow boxing, with the numerically superior Federal force invariably retreating under Washington's defensive umbrella when battle was offered. There were sharp clashes at occasional points of contact, such as Bristoe Station, Rappahannock Station, and Mine Run; however, the net result of months of hard marching and countermarching left the two armies pretty much as they had been at the start.

Lee was seriously ill in this period with heart and rheumatic problems, his condition not helped by his almost constant sparring with Richmond for reinforcements and supplies. He had lent out Longstreet's Corps with the understanding that the soldiers would be speedily returned once the western crisis had passed. "I want you badly and you cannot get back too soon," he told Longstreet just five days after his men had sealed the Chickamauga victory.[3] Yet it would not be until early April 1864 that these veterans were finally released, and late into the month before the Confederacy's disintegrating transportation system could return them to northern Virginia.

Also during this period Lee once more had to confront the increasingly serious matter of desertions from the ranks of his army.

Again he was an outspoken advocate for imposing the death penalty on those convicted of the charge. He also had to fend off a half-hearted attempt by the Confederate President to reassign him as a replacement for General Braxton Bragg in the west, a job that eventually went to Joseph E. Johnston. Then a new opponent appeared, brought in from the west, where he had delivered a series of important victories. His name was Ulysses S. Grant.

As Lee observed the enemy camps grow across the Rapidan River, he constantly tried to anticipate his opponent's next move. "Their plans are not sufficiently developed to discover them," he wrote Jefferson Davis on March 30, "but I think we can assume that if Gen[era]l Grant is to direct operations on this frontier he will concentrate a large force on one or more lines, & prudence dictates that we should make such preparations as are in our power." Lee had few more details by April 5, but was sufficiently alarmed by the continuing enemy buildup that he prophesized that the "great effort of the enemy in this campaign will be made in Virginia."[4]

Characteristically, Lee's impulse was aggressive. "If Richmond could be held secure against the attack from the east," he told Davis on April 15, "I would propose . . . to . . . move right against the enemy on the Rappahannock." This, he believed, was the only action that could upset the designs of the enemy. "Should God give us a crowning victory there," he continued, "all their plans would be dissipated."

Lee's post-Gettysburg objectives were no longer shaped by a battle of annihilation endgame. His new purpose was sketched out in a February 3 message to Davis. He at once discounted the possibility of making further movements into the north. "We are not in a condition, & never have been, in my opinion, to invade the enemy's country with a prospect of permanent benefit," he said. We can," he continued, "alarm & embarrass him to some extent & thus prevent his undertaking anything of magnitude against us."[5] Bedeviled by the usual lack of supplies and jaded cavalry, Lee was still waiting and watching when, in the early hours of May 4, 1864, news came that the massive Union army was in motion.

Two of Lee's three infantry corps were spread along the Rapidan—Richard Ewell's Second Corps men furthest east, grouped to cover Summerville Ford, and A. P. Hill's Third Corps to their west with headquarters at Orange Court House. About ten miles south of Hill were Longstreet's recently arrived men, camped around Gordonsville. By mid-morning, May 4, Lee knew enough about the enemy's likely course to begin moving his infantry toward their probable Rapidan River crossing points—Germanna and Ely's fords—Ewell following the Orange Turnpike and Hill the Orange Plank Road, with Longstreet marching northward to hook onto Hill's right.

Lee was expecting that the Federals would either turn toward him to fight or away from him to seize Fredericksburg; he was not anticipating that they would continue marching south, thus exposing their flank. He spoke of this on the evening of May 4 to his former aide, Armistead Long, who later remembered that Lee "expressed himself surprised that his new adversary had placed himself in the same predicament as 'Fighting Joe' [Hooker] had done the previous Spring. He hoped the result would be even more disastrous to Grant than that which Hooker had experienced."[6]

It was Lee's intention to bring Grant to battle, but not until he could concentrate the Army of Northern Virginia. With Longstreet at least a day's march distant, Lee had to advance his units near enough to be able to strike on May 6, but not so close as to initiate a general engagement before then. Complicating matters, Ewell's and Hill's corps were moving on parallel courses with several miles of often impenetrable wilderness between them. Fretting most about the fragile health of his Third Corps commander, Lee rode with Hill on May 4, and tried, in a message sent at 8:00 P.M., to convey his intentions to Ewell. The missive's close stated that Lee's desire was to bring the enemy to battle "as soon now as possible"; in retrospect, it seems that this communicated an unintentional urgency to his Second Corps commander.[7]

On the morning of May 5, as Ewell pugnaciously advanced his corps to within picket distance of the Federal Fifth Corps camped around Wilderness Tavern, he received a disturbing clarification from Lee (via Major Campbell Brown): Lee did not want him "to get his troops entangled so as to be unable to disengage them, in case the enemy were in force." Ewell instructed his brigadiers that they were "not to allow themselves to become involved, but to fall back slowly if pressed." This injected a near-fatal lack of resolution in these officers to hold their position, and when a portion of the line south of the Orange Turnpike was assailed around 1:00 P.M., it nearly collapsed. Writing later of these events, Major Brown declared, "I don't believe these brigades would have been so easily broken had it not been for the general understanding that we were to retire . . . if attacked in force."[8] It took a brilliant counterattack by John Gordon's Brigade, coupled with the leveling effect of the Wilderness itself, that made it possible for Ewell to reestablish his lines by 3:00 P.M.

Although accompanying Hill's column along the Orange Plank Road, Lee exercised little direct control this day. Between three and four o'clock he sent a suggestion to Major General Henry Heth that he push forward to where the east-west-running Plank Road met the north-south-running Brock Road. The one stipulation was that he do so only if he could avoid a general engagement. Heth demurred without firm orders, which Lee declined to provide. The issue became moot at 4:00 P.M. when Heth was suddenly attacked by Union troops pressing west along Plank Road. Only darkness prevented a significant Federal victory.

Lee's decisions on this critical night put his army at great risk. Even though he knew that the Third Corps had been roughly handled in the day's fighting, and was in receipt of several requests from A. P. Hill to let him regroup his scattered units, Lee insisted that the men be left undisturbed. This came after he had learned that the First Corps, which had halted its march at dusk, would not recommence moving until 1:00 A.M. It had taken the lone mounted officer more than ninety minutes to cover the distance, and Lee was now basing his plans on the assumption that a full corps, marching in the dark over unfamiliar roads, would be able to cover that distance in something approaching three hours.

U. S. Grant, on the other hand, was decidedly proactive, ordering an all-out assault for 4:30 A.M. Pressed by Army of the Potomac commander George Meade for a ninety-minute delay, Grant relented, allowing only an extra thirty minutes. It was near that appointed hour when attacks surged ahead along both roadways. In the northern sector, where Ewell's entrenched men faced portions of the Union Fifth and Sixth Corps, the Federals were beaten back without serious problem. Along Hill's disordered, unentrenched line, the results were dramatically different.

After ninety minutes of hard fighting, Hill's soldiers had been shoved back to the dozen guns of William Poague's battalion, which Lee had ordered established in a last-stand position at the Widow Tapp farm. It was at this time and place that Lee berated the men of McGowan's South Carolina Brigade for running "like a flock of geese."[9] Only the timely arrival of Longstreet's Corps as a compact striking force made it possible to blunt and then stop the Union tide. A second noteworthy incident occurred when Lee acted to personally lead Longstreet's Texas Brigade in a sacrificial counterattack. He knew well the value of his presence on a battlefield, and like any shrewd leader recognized that a little theatricality was sometimes required. His gesture did the job; the Texans attacked with great fury, taking heavy losses as they helped stall the enemy advance.

Lee had the ability to instill an aggressive spirit in his key officers, and even the sometimes hesitant Longstreet was no exception. Hardly had Lee's First Corps commander put paid to the Federal advance than he was dividing his force, sending some of it around the enemy's left flank using an unfinished railroad bed located by Lee's chief engineer. Lee used the pause while this assault was being prepared to visit with Ewell and urged him to press matters on his flank, something the one-legged general was reluctant to do. By the time Lee returned to the Orange Plank Road, Longstreet had commenced his attack.

In a remarkable similarity to Chancellorsville, Longstreet's Corps rolled up the Union flank and began collapsing it toward the center. Unlike Chancellorsville, however, there was no cascading panic in the Federal ranks, but instead a sulky retreat that went only as far as Brock Road, where a row of half-finished breastworks provided the critical nucleus for Union officers to rally their regiments.

His flankers were still battling in the woods when Longstreet advanced his main line along the Orange Plank Road. When the two came together there was confusion and a dangerous loss of momentum. With his staff and key officers, Longstreet rode forward to straighten things out and keep the attack pressing ahead. In another striking parallel to Chancellorsville, his mounted party was struck by friendly fire. Longstreet was seriously wounded and several with him were killed.

When word of this was delivered to Lee, the Confederate commander seemed wholly uninformed about affairs in the southern sector. According to one of Longstreet's staff, Lee "was not in sufficient touch with the actual position of the troops to proceed with it as [Longstreet] . . . would have been able to do."[10] For this reason, the attack begun by Longstreet was halted. In retrospect, Lee's best opportunity to smash a portion of the Union army was lost.

Lee believed that a single powerful blow at the presumably weakened and demoralized enemy would give him the success he needed to restore the Rapidan line. It took him several hours to position thirteen brigades into a striking force and send them against the Brock Road works. The Union troops (most from Hancock's

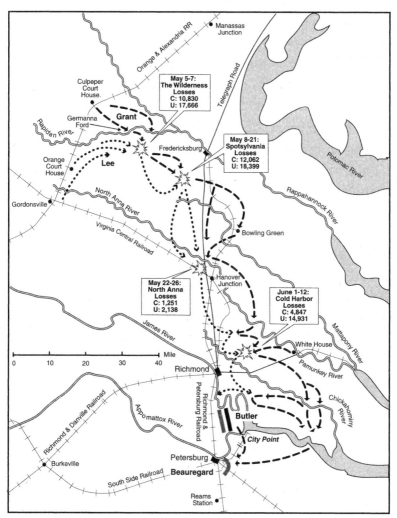

Map labels:

Manassas Junction

Orange & Alexandria RR

Telegraph Road

Culpeper Court House.

May 5-7:
The Wilderness
Losses
C: 10,830
U: 17,666

Germanna Ford

Grant

Rapidan River

Fredericksburg

May 8-21:
Spotsylvania
Losses
C: 12,062
U: 18,399

Orange Court House

Lee

Potomac River

Gordonsville

North Anna River

Rappahannock River

Virginia Central Railroad

Bowling Green

May 22-26:
North Anna
Losses
C: 1,251
U: 2,138

Hanover Junction

June 1-12:
Cold Harbor
Losses
C: 4,847
U: 14,931

James River

Mattapony River

White House

Pamunkey River

Mile
0   10   20   30   40

Richmond

Chickahominy River

Richmond & Petersburg Railroad

Appomattox River

Richmond & Danville Railroad

Butler

City Point

Burkeville

Petersburg

Beauregard

South Side Railroad

Reams Station

THE OVERLAND CAMPAIGN

hard-fighting Second Corps) used the lull to refill empty ammunition pouches and improve their defensive trenches, so that the Rebel effort was beaten back, though not without difficulty in places. On the Confederate left, a flanking attack devised by John Gordon was launched too late in the day and with too little strength to do more than sweep up a few hundred unfortunate prisoners and to start rumors among the Union soldiers of a military disaster that were decisively quashed at Grant's and Meade's headquarters.

Except for some reconnaissance probes, both sides rested during the daylight hours of May 7, though it was a deceptive quiet. U. S. Grant issued orders for the Union army to change position after dark; new objective: Spotsylvania Court House. At the same time Lee sifted through fragmentary reports of the Federal activity that supported several different interpretations. The Union army might be retreating toward Fredericksburg or moving on to Spotsylvania. (Federal engineers had removed the pontoon bridges across the Rapidan, eliminating the possibility that Grant's men would retrace their steps.) Although Lee biographer Douglas Southall Freeman believed that the general correctly read Grant's mind by ordering his First Corps (now under Major General Richard H. Anderson) to Spotsylvania, the evidence strongly suggests that he underestimated his opponent's resolve to fight it out on this line of advance.

Lee's orders sending Anderson south did not impart any urgency to the act, and they were discretionary regarding starting time, allowing him until 3:00 A.M., May 8, to get started. It was Anderson's own decision (likely motivated by a desire to make a good showing in his first outing as a corps commander) to depart at 10:00 P.M., May 7, and the pure chance that his route took him through still-burning woods, precluding any rest stops, that accounts for his timely arrival at Spotsylvania mere minutes ahead of the Federal vanguard. As late as the morning of May 8, Lee, still in the Wilderness, was telling Richmond that the "enemy had abandoned his position and is moving toward Fredericksburg."[11]

Once alerted to the danger posed by the Federal advance, Lee ordered the other units still in the Wilderness to hurry to Anderson's aid, and then headed south, reaching Spotsylvania in the early afternoon. By this time the most significant Federal thrust had been stopped by Anderson's infantry and the cavalry under Major General Fitzhugh Lee. Robert E. Lee arrived to witness across the slope of Laurel Hill the final attacks of the day, a poorly coordinated effort by portions of the enemy's Fifth and Sixth Corps that was in turn defeated by the fortuitous arrival of Ewell's Corps.

Lee faced an even greater challenge to the army's core command structure. The badly wounded Longstreet was gone for the rest of the summer, Ewell was clearly showing the strain of the campaign and barely holding up, and then word arrived that A. P. Hill was too ill to continue running his corps. Jubal Early was put in temporary charge, but Lee had to proceed knowing that two-thirds of his top officers were out of action.

The next few days at Spotsylvania saw him reacting to a series of aggressive moves by Grant. On the night of May 9, the Federal Second Corps tried to swing around his left flank, but it was slow crossing the Po River and was already falling back when struck the next day by a counterattack, resulting in the noteworthy loss of two of Hancock's cannon. May 10 also saw a series of frontal assaults against the entrenched Confederate lines that stretched east from Brock Road, bulged out into a salient, then twisted back toward the south to shield the court house village. The Yankee attacks undertaken by the Fifth and Second Corps were repulsed with loss to the enemy, but one storming party, a hand-picked column led by Colonel Emory Upton, punched through Confederate trenches along the salient's western face and only failed for want of support.

The relative ease with which Lee's men had stopped these heavy assaults was a tribute to their stalwart fighting spirit, the force multiplier that entrenchments gave those holding them, and Lee's superb eye for defensible terrain. Yet he let stand a decision by a subordinate to deploy his troops into a vulnerable salient. The position, created during the evening and night of May 8–9 by Edward Johnson's Division of Ewell's Corps, jutted a good half mile out from the tight curve of the rest of the line. Lee's chief engineer, Major General Martin Luther Smith, thought it could be held if strongly packed with artillery. Lee agreed, but at least one of the artillerists sent into the salient declared that it was "a wretchedly defective line."[12]

During the cold and rainy night of May 11, Lee was told of many men moving behind the enemy's position. Enemy activity was reported on the Confederate left and even more on its right. Yet Lee's crystal ball remained clouded. He said to Henry Heth, "My opinion is the enemy are preparing to retreat tonight to Fredericksburg. I wish you to have everything in readiness to pull out at a moment's notice, but do not disturb your artillery, until you commence moving. We must attack these people if they retreat."[13]

However, Lee reversed himself a very short time afterward, following a meeting with General Ewell and his staff, where, according to Major Campbell Brown, he told his Second Corps commander "to withdraw from the trenches and . . . to do the same with the artillery."[14] Only after Ewell protested that his men would be better off spending this raw night in the relative comfort of their trench bunkers did Lee relent enough to delay execution of the infantry movement order until morning.

However, anticipating muddy road delays, the guns in the salient kept on the original schedule, so when the drizzly dawn of May 12 arrived and nearly 20,000 Union soldiers pounded out of the mist in a grand assault, only a handful of cannon opposed them. Once he learned of the enemy's attack, Lee realized he had made a terrible miscalculation. Nothing but hard fighting and personal leadership could salvage the situation.

First with John Gordon's men, and then with Nathaniel Harris's Mississippians, Lee rode to the head of an advancing column as if to lead it into the chaotic combat ahead. It was indeed rare for him to act in such a public manner. Whether it was a personal offering of his life for mistakes made, or something calculated to inspire troops facing deadly assignments, he made the gesture and his soldiers responded with a will. Both attacks landed sharp hard blows against the attacking Federal masses, and both commands suffered grievous losses doing so.

Had the corresponding actions planned by Grant against the flanks of the Confederate position been driven home with half the determination shown in the center, even Lee's symbolic acts would have been for naught. But Ambrose Burnside's inept handling of his assignment to press from the east with the Ninth Corps and Gouverneur K. Warren's refusal to add to the body count of the Fifth Corps on Laurel Hill allowed Lee to pour reinforcements into the embattled salient. These costly counterattacks, coupled with an almost complete breakdown of tactical cohesion among the Union forces involved, allowed Lee's desperate fighters to halt, then reverse the Federal gains.

It is to Lee's credit that by midday he recognized the diminishing returns involved in trying to restore a badly sited position. He hurried to complete a shorter line of works crossing the salient's narrow neck, into which he moved his troops early on May 13. Though Grant's steamroller assault had virtually eliminated a division of Lee's army, it had not broken his lines.

The news got worse for Lee. Most of his cavalry and its incomparable chief, Major General Jeb Stuart, had ridden out two days earlier in pursuit of a large Union raiding force under Major General Philip H. Sheridan that was maneuvering against Richmond.

Stuart successfully blocked Sheridan in a melee near Yellow Tavern, but at the cost of his own life. "He never brought me a piece of false information," Lee said when first told of the loss, later adding, "I can scarcely think of him without weeping."[15]

He spent the next few days reorganizing his battered command structure and deftly parrying Federal probing attacks. His appeals to Richmond for extra troops were met with excuses from Jefferson Davis. A subsidiary action ordered as part of Grant's grand design saw Major General Benjamin Butler's Army of the James threaten the Confederate capital from its southern side, via a peninsula formed by the James and Appomattox rivers known as Bermuda Hundred. Rebel defenses in this section were under the overall command of General P. G. T. Beauregard, who refused to release any of his units to Lee. (Only when the Army of the Potomac drew even nearer to Richmond did Jefferson Davis see any merit to Lee's requests.)

The Army of the Potomac began to sidle away from Spotsylvania beginning late in the evening of May 20, a process that took nearly a full day to complete. In the evening of May 21, once Lee was certain that the Federals were not feinting, he put his own troops on roads heading toward Richmond. His army's destination was the North Anna River. During the campaigns of Fredericksburg, Chancellorsville, and even Gettysburg, Lee had considered the river's south bank a naturally strong fall back position. Now he was counting on its defensive strengths to help him arrest the inexorable advance of Grant's army.

Lee's ride there was an exhausting one. The stress and pressures on him were exacting a cruel toll on his health and acuity. Early on the morning of May 22, he paused near Dickinson's Mill on the Telegraph Road to send an explanation to President Davis why he was ceding so much territory to the Federals without a fight. He cited the difficult terrain ("a wooded country . . . where nothing is known beyond what can be ascertained by feeling")[16] and his worry that Sheridan's cavalry might yet strike for the Confederate capital.

In a letter written the next day to his wife, Lee put down some additional reasons: "We have the advantage of being nearer our supplies & less liable to have our communication . . . cut by his cavalry & he is getting farther from his base."[17]

Yet, despite the hard evidence of his recent clashes with Grant, Lee reached the North Anna convinced he had won some breathing space. He told his corps commanders to rest their men and did not mention preparing any defensive positions. So it must have been with a mixture of surprise, resignation, and fatalism that he watched from the porch of the Ellington House as thin lines of Yankee skirmishers aggressively pushed down the Telegraph Road toward the North Anna early on May 23.

Whatever hope Lee may have had of holding the river line was gone by nightfall, when he found out that the Federals had successfully crossed upstream near Jericho Mill. Misled by poor scouting intelligence that grossly underestimated the enemy's numbers, A. P. Hill (returned to Third Corps command) sent a division to tackle what turned out to be a full Union corps. His soldiers were unable to prevent this crossing, which effectively flanked Lee's line along the river bank. Something of Lee's frustration over this turn of events boiled out during his angry debriefing of Hill. "Why did you not do as [Stonewall] Jackson would have done—thrown your whole force upon these people and driven them back?" he demanded of his Third Corps commander.[18]

Lee's health continued to worsen; still, he met with his officers that night to try to salvage the situation. Out of the discussion came an idea that offered the real possibility of disrupting the enemy's plans. Lee realigned his army and set his men to digging a fresh line of earthworks. The new position was generally in a V shape, with its point pinned to high ground along the North Anna's south bank at Ox Ford. The two wings of the V ran southward to natural anchors, creating an open arena east and west of the position into which Lee hoped to lure the Federals.

Once the enemy wings crossed the river they would divide on the point of the V and be separated from each other, with Lee's compact force between them. Taking advantage of his strong entrenchments, he planned to leave a minimum force holding one flank of the V, while the bulk of his army attacked the Federals opposite the other. In this manner his numerically inferior army would overwhelm a smaller and isolated portion of Grant's larger force.

North Anna should have been the tactical victory Lee had sought in the Wilderness and Spotsylvania, an opportunity to "fall upon them unexpectedly [and] . . . derange their plans." The grand attack never took place, however. According to Lee's staff officer, Colonel Charles Venable, "In the midst of these operations on the North Anna, General Lee was taken sick and confined to his tent. As he lay prostrated by his sickness, he would often repeat: 'We must strike them a blow—We must never let them pass us again.'"[19] It is a powerful vignette, one that says much about Lee's mental and physical condition at this time.

At last recognizing the trap, Grant halted the advance and ordered soldiers time to dig their own entrenchments, so in a short while they were well protected against any Confederate attack. It does not bode well for the Army of Northern Virginia that Lee apparently felt that he could trust none of his corps commanders—Anderson, Ewell, Hill—to manage this operation. How else can one explain the fact that the moment he was rendered hors de combat the plan died stillborn?

Grant pulled his force back across the North Anna, then continued its movement around Lee's right flank by advancing along the far bank of the Pamunkey River. To counter this, the ailing Confederate commander (now traveling in a carriage) positioned his army near Richmond at Atlee's Station. There he waited to see where Grant intended to turn toward the capital. There was another crisis in his command when Richard Ewell reported himself too ill to continue. Lee immediately put Jubal Early in Ewell's place, making the change official on May 29.

Thus far in this relentless campaign, Lee had to deal with personnel changes atop all three of his corps, three of his divisions, and fourteen of his brigades. Moreover, he still had to find someone to replace the fallen Stuart. When his own health problems are added to the mix, his misreadings of circumstances in the days to come are understandable. Lee was losing his edge. In a letter to his wife written on May 29, he expressed the fervent hope that "God will give me strength for all He wishes me to do."[20]

On May 28, when major units of the Union and Confederate cavalry clashed near Haw's Shop, east of Richmond, Lee knew that the Army of the Potomac was coming across the Pamunkey River near Hanovertown. Upon receipt of this intelligence, he posted two corps across the enemy's direct route in a north-south line behind the protective marshes of Totopotomoy Creek.

Newly promoted Jubal Early was quick to demonstrate his own Lee-like fondness for the offensive. On May 30 he led his command around the left flank of the Union line, striking it near Bethesda Church. A combination of faulty coordination with other Southern units, poor tactical field management on Early's part, and the presence of a Federal general (Gouverneur K. Warren) who thrived from fighting on the defensive resulted in nearly 1,200 Confederate casualties for no corresponding gain in position or intelligence.

Even as Early's troops were engaged, Lee was informed that a contingent of enemy infantry brought up from Butler's army on Bermuda Hundred had landed at White House, fifteen miles below Hanovertown. The roads led west from that point, like a dagger slipping in under his right flank. A rapid march by these Union troops would threaten his rear and possibly even cut him off from Richmond.

The events of the next four days, May 31–June 3, showed only too clearly that while the offensive power of the Army of Northern

Virginia may have bled out during the Overland Campaign, its defensive abilities remained unimpaired. On June 1 Lee was able to effect a junction between a portion of his army (Anderson's Corps) and troops that he had finally pried away from Beauregard (Major General Robert F. Hoke's Division) in order to secure a strategically important crossroads near Cold Harbor. Through a foul-up on the Union side, the troops that landed at White House had marched in the wrong direction, so the only soldiers wearing blue at Cold Harbor were lightly armed cavalrymen under Phil Sheridan.

It was a precious opportunity to bloody Grant's nose. Once more however, inept cooperation among the Confederate forces, and a tactical error by Anderson in allowing a large and raw South Carolina regiment to spearhead his attack, made it possible for Sheridan's fast-firing troopers to hold on long enough for infantry supports to arrive. Unable to dislodge the reinforced enemy, Lee's men began to entrench, but under a heavy enemy assault later in the day they ceded sections of their position near Cold Harbor.

The Yankee follow-up attack expected for June 2 did not materialize, though not for want of effort. An advance had been ordered by Grant, who picked his favorite shock force—Hancock's Second Corps—to lead. But that meant a long night march for these soldiers, not enough of whom arrived in time on June 2 to mount the operation. Grant rescheduled the action for June 3. Lee's men used the unexpected respite to deadly advantage, laying out a defensive position that created a nearly perfect killing ground in its front.

The Confederate defensive victory that followed on June 3 at Cold Harbor was more a product of the almost innate ability of Lee's men to dig and defend than the result of any planning by Lee. Indeed, reading the brief report he sent to Richmond that evening, one is tempted to conclude that he was as surprised as his soldiers at their easy win. "Our loss today has been small, and our success, under the blessing of God, all that we could expect," he noted.[21]

As matters along this front settled into a spiteful stalemate, Lee's attention was drawn to the Shenandoah Valley, where a Confederate advantage won at the battle of New Market on May 15 was jeopardized by the arrival of a 20,000-man-strong Yankee army under Major General David Hunter. Writing on June 6 to Jefferson Davis, Lee urged that "some good officer should be sent into the Valley at once to take command there and collect all the forces, . . . & endeavor to drive the enemy out."[22] He reluctantly offered to return the small force of 2,100 he had borrowed from that theater, but pointedly did not mention the possibility of supplying any more. Three days later Lee confirmed reports that a large body of cavalry under Sheridan had left Grant's army on June 7 and was likely marching to link up with Hunter's army. He also indicated that two of his own cavalry divisions—Major General Wade Hampton's and Fitzhugh Lee's—were pursuing Sheridan.

By June 11 Lee was under heavy pressure from Richmond to turn things around in the Shenandoah Valley. A message sent that day revealed the dilemma he faced. He reckoned that it would take a full corps to alter the balance of forces there, and he fully realized that there was just one army close enough to supply it. Expecting orders to do so from Richmond, Lee pointed out the huge risks of his detaching so many of his men. "If it is deemed prudent to hazard the defense of Richmond, the interests involved by thus diminishing the force here, I will do so," he said. "I think this is what the enemy would desire."[23] His arguments were unavailing. On the morning of June 13, a reduced version of his Ewell's Corps under Jubal Early departed for the Shenandoah Valley.

While Lee saw no way to attack Grant as long as he was entrenched at Cold Harbor, he did hope to find an advantage when Grant tried to shift his great army. On June 4 he advised Richard Anderson that should the enemy commence to change position, the automatic response would be "to move down and attack him with our whole force."[24] To this end he urged the officer to keep especially vigilant in order to provide a timely warning. Anderson in response sent a circular to his commands stressing that "General Lee is exceedingly anxious to be advised of any movement the enemy may undertake."[25] To Jubal Early Lee had confided, "We must destroy this army of Grant's before he gets to the James River. If he gets there, it will become a siege, and then it will be a mere question of time."[26]

Even as he was looking for a chance to catch Grant's army in the open, Richmond was being bombarded by messages from Beauregard demanding the recall of all troops temporarily transferred to Lee. Writing at 9:30 A.M. on June 9 from his headquarters north of Petersburg, Beauregard reported a Union attack on the Cockade City. "The return soon as possible of my troops sent to General Lee is again urged on War Department," Beauregard said.[27] Although Beauregard's partisans would later blame Lee for failing to respond quickly to the mounting threats against Petersburg, Lee biographer Douglas Southall Freeman's analysis of the communications traffic supports his thesis that Lee gave Beauregard all the help that general sought.

Personnel matters also vied for Lee's attention. Richard Ewell indicated that he was well enough to resume command of his corps, about to march into the Shenandoah Valley. Skeptical of Ewell's ability to perform well in a vigorous campaign and to manage independent operations, on June 12 Lee tactfully recommended that since the officer had not fully recovered it would be best if he were assigned to direct Richmond's defenses (which he was).

Then, on the morning of June 13, Lee awoke to learn that Grant's army had yet again given him the slip during the night. Save for a few rear guards, the huge Yankee army was gone from his front. Just as after Chancellorsville, Lee saw his best opportunity to strike a blow lost because his subordinates had failed him. According to Eppa Hunton, one of George Pickett's brigadiers, "It was said that General Lee was in a furious passion—one of the few times during the war. When he did get mad he was mad all over."[28]

Two years earlier, when in a similar situation facing McClellan and enjoying better odds, Lee had pressed an aggressive pursuit of the enemy marching to the James River. This time, however, he held back, allowing only the most tenuous contact between the two forces. Why he was suddenly so reluctant to strike with everything he had speaks to a fundamental shift in his goals and objectives. With a decisive enemy defeat no longer possible, Lee was looking to the repudiation of Lincoln's war policies in the North's fall elections. For the South to have a bargaining position with any new U.S. government it needed a credible military presence, so Lee's impulse now was to preserve his force and take fewer risks. His offensive operations were mostly in the nature of counterattacks aimed at restoring ground lost, not eliminating the enemy.

Lee's unwillingness to press Grant's army as it marched to the James allowed the Federal general to patch together a strike force from Butler's and Meade's armies that he threw against Petersburg, fully confident that the vital railroad hub would fall into his hands. It didn't. Inept Union tactical leadership, a brilliant defense stage-managed by Beauregard, and the cumulative effect of the terrible attrition suffered since May by the Army of the Potomac allowed Petersburg's hard-pressed defenders to hold until the Army of Northern Virginia arrived.

By the time Lee showed up in person, on June 18, the Federal high tide had passed. When an ebullient Beauregard pressed Lee with plans for a counterstroke, the Confederate chieftain demurred. According to Beauregard's staff officer Alfred Roman, "General Lee refused his assent, on the ground that his troops needed rest, and that the defensive having been thus far so advantageous to him against Grant's offensive . . . at Petersburg, he preferred continuing the same mode of warfare."[29]

Grant held the initiative and did not hesitate to maintain it, often to the detriment of the worn-down Army of the Potomac. Lee took an opportunistic posture and reacted quickly to any Federal incursion. On June 22, a Union column attempting to extend Grant's trenches across the Weldon Railroad south of Petersburg was sent tumbling back to its starting point by a timely flank attack. Immediately after that fight, Lee met with the chief of artillery for the First Corps, E. P. Alexander, to see if they could not break the Union stranglehold on the Cockade City. The two found an area where the Union right rested on the south bank Appomattox, and where it was flanked by Confederate positions on the higher opposite bank. Lee and Alexander devised a plan to pummel those positions with artillery fire, then attack with infantry to roll up the line as far south as possible.

Since operational control along the Petersburg lines belonged to Beauregard, Lee had to convince the officer to sign on to the plan and then stand back to let him execute it. The scheme required commingling units from Lee's command (in this case, Major General Charles Field's Division) with troops from Beauregard (Hoke's Division). The integration of the two forces was no more successful than that which had been tried on June 1 at Cold Harbor. Alexander did pull off his part by providing a powerful artillery barrage. According to a Northern reporter present, with the "exception of Gettysburg, the war has not afforded another instance of so many guns concentrated upon one point and firing so rapidly for such a length of time."[30] Hoke and Field failed to mesh their actions so badly, that the leading units in the attack (from Hagood's South Carolina brigade) were trapped in no-man's-land without support, resulting in many being captured. Reviewing the action afterward, Lee commented that there "seems to have been some misunderstanding as to the part each division was expected to have performed."[31] A more personal spin was provided by Lee's staff officer, Charles Venable, who concluded, "And thus the whole plan, so well conceived and so successful in its beginning, was given up to the sorrow of the commanding general."[32]

Knowing full well that his opponent could not ignore a threat to Richmond, Grant took advantage of his interior lines to constantly split Lee's attention between his capital and Petersburg. Lee's acute sensitivity to his Richmond flank was made evident on July 26 when Grant landed an expedition at Deep Bottom consisting of Hancock's Second Corps accompanied by two divisions of Sheridan's cavalry. Shackled by Hancock's lackluster leadership (a Gettysburg wound was progressively debilitating him) and Sheridan's near indifference to his assignment, the operation accomplished little before withdrawing on July 29. By then, however, Lee had taken the bait.

At the time Grant's movement began, Rebel defenses north of the James consisted of elements of Major General Joseph B. Kershaw's Division (Anderson's Corps) and a portion of Major General Cadmus Wilcox's Division (Hill's Corps). Responding to Grant's move, Lee dispatched all of Heth's Division and two of his cavalry divisions from Petersburg, leaving behind just three infantry divisions to hold back three enemy corps. That Grant was unable to capitalize on this great advantage at the Battle of the Crater is a sad story best told elsewhere.

Lee's next Petersburg counterstroke occurred after Beauregard proved unable to eliminate an August 18 Union lodgment on the Weldon Railroad; that was then maintained in the face of fierce counterattacks lasting three days. (Beauregard would be gone in a month, transferred to oversee North Carolina's defenses at Lee's suggestion.) Grant immediately sought to exploit his hard-won advantage by sending portions of Hancock's corps south along the rail line to wreck it. Unlike the previous occasions, when Confederate scouts seriously underestimated the size of the Union force, this time the Southern patrols under the able leadership of Wade

Hampton delivered accurate intelligence regarding the size and disposition of the Federals.

It was Hampton who suggested that the Yankee track wreckers were far enough from the heavily entrenched Federal lines to be vulnerable to a combined cavalry-infantry strike. Lee was hesitant at first, believing that it was just too risky to send such a force so far outside his own earthworks, but after a little reflection he changed his mind. If he didn't do something, the Yankees would rip up the tracks as far as the North Carolina border, significantly lengthening his remaining road and rail supply links, and greatly increasing the difficulties of maintaining his defense of Petersburg and Richmond. Even then Lee was cautious, assigning only one infantry division to accompany Hampton. However, Lee was the kind of gambler who, once he had pushed his chips onto the table, was more likely to raise the stakes rather than leave the game. He eventually added additional portions of two other divisions to the force and placed A. P. Hill in overall command.

Alerted to their danger, Hancock's Federals hastily took up a poorly sited defensive position near Reams Station. It was there, on the afternoon of August 25, that Hill attacked them. The first assaults were thrown back, but a panic in one of Hancock's exhausted regiments allowed the attackers to penetrate the defenses to collapse the perimeter. Reams Station was a substantial Confederate victory resulting in Federal losses of more than 2,600 (most captured) to a Confederate cost of 720. It stopped Union efforts to further disrupt Petersburg's remaining supply arteries, boosted Confederate morale, and bought Lee more time.

Lee's investment of men in the Shenandoah Valley initially paid off, thanks to Jubal Early's risky belligerence. It took four days for Early's veterans to march and ride as far as Lynchburg, where they promptly scattered the Union force under Major General David Hunter that had so frightened Richmond. By mid-July Early had proceeded into Maryland, and by July 11 his men were outside

Washington after scattering a smaller force under Major General Lew A. Wallace that had tried to halt them along the Monocacy River outside Frederick, Maryland. Early found Washington's defenses much too large for his small army, so he returned to the Valley, where he fought and beat a 9,500-man enemy detachment at Kernstown on July 24.

Early was doing everything that Lee had hoped when he sent him; he was taking attention from Petersburg, protecting the Shenandoah granaries, and diverting U.S. military assets from going to the James River front. The balance began to shift on August 1 when Grant appointed Philip Sheridan to oppose Early. Along with Sheridan, Grant sent two divisions of cavalry from the Army of the Potomac at Petersburg, units that departed via steamers on August 4. It was an adroit move by Grant, since mounted units had little role to play among the miles of earthworks between Richmond and Petersburg. The flotilla of thirty-six transports was spotted by Confederate scouts, who reported the same to Lee.

Suddenly his bet had been called and raised; it was now up to him to see it or fold. "I fear that this force is intended to operate against General Early," Lee informed Jefferson Davis that day, "and when added to that already opposed to him, may be more than he can manage."[33] He met with Davis and Richard H. Anderson in Richmond on August 6. The decision was made to detach from his command one infantry division (Major General Joseph B. Kershaw's), an artillery battalion (Lieutenant Colonel Wilfred E. Cutshaw's), and a cavalry division (Fitzhugh Lee's) to reinforce Early. On August 11 Lee raised the stakes again by ordering Wade Hampton to take another cavalry division to the Valley.

Lee believed that his sending of reinforcements to the Valley would prompt Grant to do the same. According to Fitzhugh Lee, Robert E. Lee's ultimate purpose was "to induce Grant to send troops to Sheridan equivalent to [a] . . . whole corps. In that case Lee would again re-enforce Early and transfer the principal scene of hostilities to the Potomac."[34] Once more, however, Lee seriously misread his opponent. Grant's response was not to send more men to Sheridan, but to order another expedition to threaten Richmond.

Grant's second Deep Bottom expedition was again entrusted to the ailing Hancock—who this time had infantry units from the Tenth Corps added to his forces. This new operation began on August 13. Hancock's plan was similar to the first: a turning movement by the troops landing near Deep Bottom, pushing along the east bank of Bailey's Creek, and swinging in toward Richmond along either the Darbytown or Charles City roads. In an eerie echo of previous events, Union command leadership was ambiguous in its goals, tentative in its execution, and unsuccessful in its efforts.

An incident involving Lee during this operation throws more light on his character. According to a Georgia soldier named John C. Reed, the general was positioned in the rear of the Rebel battle lines when a Federal advance caused some Confederate units to break and run. Reed recalled how Lee rode among the stragglers rushing from the front and spoke to each one, "harshly demanding that he show his wound." When a tall soldier, hat tightly pulled down over his eyes, failed to comply, the general "showed great anger and hemmed the man by wheeling his horse across him." Lee again commanded that the soldier show blood. This time the man raised his hat to reveal an ugly wound. Lee, remembered Reed, "did not apologize for his injurious words, but he told him where he could find some water near, and bade him go there forthwith and bathe his forehead well."[35]

Grant's regular forays north of the James River were sorely limiting Lee's options. He decided to mount an offensive aimed at clearing the river's north bank once and for all of the Yankee interlopers. Working with a hastily recalled Wade Hampton, he drew up what one historian of this campaign has called "an ambitious plan to drive Hancock's force back to the river."[36] Hampton's riders were to flank the Federal position and then, supported by infantry, roll

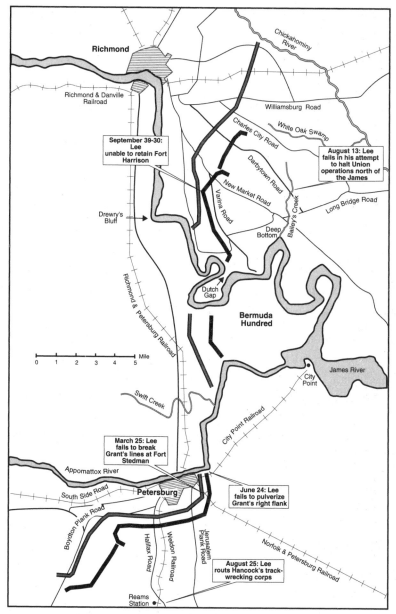

Richmond

Richmond & Danville Railroad

Chickahominy River

Williamsburg Road

White Oak Swamp

Charles City Road

September 39-30: Lee unable to retain Fort Harrison

Darbytown Road

August 13: Lee fails in his attempt to halt Union operations north of the James

New Market Road

Long Bridge Road

Varina Road

Bailey's Creek

Drewry's Bluff

Deep Bottom

Dutch Gap

Bermuda Hundred

0 1 2 3 4 5 Mile

Richmond & Petersburg Railroad

James River

City Point

Swift Creek

City Point Railroad

March 25: Lee fails to break Grant's lines at Fort Stedman

Appomattox River

June 24: Lee fails to pulverize Grant's right flank

South Side Road

Petersburg

Boydton Plank Road

Halifax Road

Weldon Railroad

Jerusalem Plank Road

Norfolk & Petersburg Railroad

August 25: Lee routs Hancock's track-wrecking corps

Reams Station

RICHMOND—PETERSBURG

up the line. Nothing went as planned. Through a combination of miscues and poor communication, the cavalry attack did not get under way until nearly six hours after it had been scheduled to begin. The synchronized infantry assault waited until it was too dark to be effective. Fighting ceased at dusk, ending another of Lee's counteroffensive designs. By dawn, August 21, most of the Federals had withdrawn, but Grant still retained his foothold at Deep Bottom.

Both Lee and Grant understood the two-edged value of entrenchments. While they made it possible for relatively small numbers of men to hold back many times their strength, they also allowed an offensive-minded general to mass unemployed troops into mobile columns that were then free to operate outside the earthworks. Although the Union campaign against Petersburg is often referred to as a siege, there was never a complete encirclement, so Lee always had to worry about two widely separated flanks—one below Petersburg, the other outside Richmond.

Lee's gamble to weaken himself at Richmond and Petersburg in order to support Early in the Valley failed simply because Sheridan and Grant recognized the move for what it was. Sheridan bided his time, patiently sitting on the defensive, knowing that sooner or later Lee would call back his troops. Indeed, on September 15, the expected orders were issued and Lee's reinforcements began marching south. Four days later Sheridan and Early met in battle outside Winchester, inaugurating a series of engagements that would spell the end of Lee's Valley strategy. By the end of the month he would have to send Kershaw's men back north, not to secure a victory, but to stave off impending defeat.

Lee's earlier worry that sooner or later the enemy would find a general he couldn't understand was coming true. Despite Early's protests that he was badly outnumbered, Lee did not believe Grant could transfer so many men from Petersburg without seriously curtailing his operations. He also underestimated the number of other U.S. troops available for service in the Valley. At the time he was guessing that Sheridan fielded around 12,000 soldiers; the actual count was nearly double that. Pressured by Lee to deliver some victories, Early gambled on one big October battle at Cedar Creek. The result was a decisive defeat for the Southern cause. In the end, it was Lee's fatal half measures and indecision during the latter phase of the Valley campaign that contributed to that disaster, causing what modern historian Richard J. Sommers branded "one of the worst miscalculations he ever made."[37] By mid-November Lee had had enough. He ordered back to Petersburg the remnants of Kershaw's Division and what remained of the Second Corps, now commanded by John B. Gordon after Jubal Early's resignation.

It was Grant who gained the advantage by playing the Valley game. Upon learning of Sherdian's victory over Early at Fisher's Hill on September 22–23, he advanced by one week an offensive he had planned in order to prevent Lee from dispatching any more troops there. The resulting operation, while marginally successful outside Petersburg, broke the pattern north of the James when, on September 29, troops from Butler's Army of the James stormed and captured Fort Harrison, one of the major bastions in Richmond's outer defensive ring.

Lack of manpower and the increasingly lengthy defensive line forced Lee to almost automatically cede an enemy breakthrough and then to try to reclaim the lost ground by hurriedly mounted counterattacks. In a September 2 letter to Jefferson Davis, he explained the further danger this caused, saying, "As matters now stand we have no troops disposable to meet movements of the enemy or strike when opportunity presents, without taking them from the trenches and exposing some important point."[38] He orchestrated several efforts to retake Fort Harrison, but none succeeded. As Sommers summed it up, "Counterpunching, striking back, looking—hoping—for an opening and all the while trying to fend off the Northerners' blows: To such measures was Lee now reduced."[39]

Lee's hopes that the North would weary enough of war's stalemate to talk peace were dashed by solid Union victories elsewhere: at Mobile Bay on August 5, and Atlanta on September 3. Lincoln's subsequent reelection presented Lee with one of the most difficult situations a military leader can face—the realization that the only possible resolution to the conflict would have to originate in the political sphere and not on the battlefield. Having accepted that he could not deliver situation-changing victories to the Confederate cause, was it Lee's duty to press for a compromise settlement to end the conflict, or should he narrowly limit his responsibilities to a purely military function, thus allowing the purposeless fighting to drag on? Clifford Dowdey, one of Lee's modern biographers, put it this way: "Lee was being forced into a dilemma as to the nature of his duty—to the constituted authority who legally represented the falling country or to the men who looked to him for leadership."[40]

Other issues arose during this period that provide additional insights into Lee's nature. Mostly because his army had either been moving on the offensive or holding ground some distance from Richmond, he had had no reason to consider deploying land mines, or, as they were then called, torpedoes. There were those in high command who viewed any use of these infernal devices as antithetical to the moral conduct of war. There is no evidence that Lee had given them much thought before late 1864. Now, the imperative need to hold longer and longer lines with fewer men quickly brought him around to appreciate their utility value, so on his watch torpedoes were employed in large numbers outside Richmond. In this case, pragmatism trumped another ethical concern.

Lee, whose entire prewar experiences with blacks were almost entirely as slaves, also had to confront the reality of colored soldiers opposing him. In mid-October 1864, reports reached Federals outside Richmond that captured African American infantrymen were being employed as laborers to strengthen Confederate earthworks. Utilizing soldier prisoners in such military support roles was clearly against the rules of war, so the officer commanding that front, Benjamin Butler, filed an official protest. When his communication was ignored, Butler used a group of Rebel prisoners in the same capacity and had them working directly under long-range Confederate artillery fire at Dutch Gap.

With a cycle of retaliation in the offing, Lee sent Grant a letter on October 19 to defuse the situation. In it, he made a distinction between escaped slaves in uniform, whom the Confederacy deemed lost property to be returned to proper owners, and free blacks who "are regarded as prisoners of war."[41] The former Lee proposed to employ well beyond the range of Federal guns, the latter (a few of whom, he said, were set to work by mistake) would go to a POW camp. This provided sufficient grounds for both sides to back down (Butler returned his impressed workers to their prison pens) and the issue was allowed to fade from attention.

Perhaps the most significant effort at this late date to negotiate an end to the war took place on February 3, 1865, at the so-called Hampton Roads Conference. The initiative for the talks had come from a northern public figure named Francis P. Blair Sr., who had a harebrained scheme to unite the warring factions in a common expedition against French forces in Mexico. Blair's mission was used by both Lincoln and Davis to open a channel for their own political ends. Lincoln's objective appears to have been a serious effort to present the leaders of the Confederacy with advantageous economic terms to end their secession. Davis's was a more cynical manipulation of the process aimed at reinvigorating the Southern will to fight by painting the North's policy as one of unconditional surrender. Davis guaranteed that the talks would fail by refusing to allow his three commissioners to even discuss the possibility of rejoining the Union, a point that Lincoln had said from the beginning had to be on the table.

Lee played no role in the talks, and it was through a personal intervention by U. S. Grant that a preconference impasse was broken and the sides brought together. As a part of his larger effort to recharge the Southern fighting spirit, Davis also acceded to Congressional pressure by appointing Lee commander-in-chief of all Confederate armies. It was a hollow, self-serving gesture. Said a Texas soldier of Lee's new position: "Now it was too late; the Confederacy was gasping for breath, its armies were scattered, disorganized, and, practically, commanderless, and there was not time to gather together and weld the fragments into fighting machines."[42] A staff officer added that Lee's promotion was a "mockery of rank no longer of any value."[43]

Lee did play a role in an effort by a few military men on each side to pause the war long enough to give peace a chance. This time the initiative came from the Federal general E. O. C. Ord (commanding the Army of the James following Butler's dismissal), who, on February 21, met between the lines with his pre-war friend James Longstreet (who had ended his convalescence in mid-October). Ord proposed a military convention, a cease-fire to allow politicians time to negotiate. Longstreet passed Ord's proposal up the chain of command all the way to Richmond, where, on February 22, Lee was authorized to write Grant to suggest a meeting to discuss such a convention.

Lee was enough of a political realist to know that as long as there was no give on the Southern side there would be no discussions. "My belief is that [Grant] . . . will consent to no terms, unless coupled with the condition of our return to the Union," he told Davis on March 2.[44] Lee was not far wrong. Grant had forwarded Ord's proposal onto his superiors and was promptly instructed to have "no conference with General Lee, unless it be for . . . some minor and purely military matter."[45]

It was in this context that Lee met with Confederate congressman Robert M. T. Hunter. According to Hunter, Lee indicated that "if I [Hunter] thought there was a chance for any peace which would secure better terms than were likely to be given after a surrender at discretion, he thought it my duty to make the effort." Lee rejected Hunter's request that he publicly support any such initiative, since "it would be almost equivalent to surrender." The Congressman pressed Lee to at least make a personal appeal directly to Jefferson Davis. Said Hunter, "To this he made no reply. In the whole of this conversation he never said to me he thought the chances were over; but the tone and tenor of his remarks made that impression on my mind."[46]

Lee's official dispatches in the early months of 1865 provide evidence of his increasingly bleak outlook and the mounting problems facing him. On January 27 he felt compelled to call the attention of Secretary of War Seddon to "the alarming frequency of desertions from the army." A follow-up message on February 8 catalogued the poor food and lack of clothing in the Army of Northern Virginia. "If some change is not made and the Commissary Department reorganized, I apprehend dire results," he declared.[47] Lee's petition was belatedly given full consideration. The Commissary Department was overhauled, the officer in charge was replaced, and the supply situation noticeably improved.

Eleven days later, after pondering Sherman's seemingly unstoppable march through the Carolinas, Lee concluded, "I fear it may be necessary to abandon all our cities, & preparation should be made for this contingency." Then, on March 9, in an assessment of the overall situation to John C. Breckinridge, newly appointed Secretary of War, Lee concluded that "the legitimate military consequences of [the enemy's numerical and material] . . . superiority have been postponed longer than we had reason to anticipate."[48]

Discussing military options with one of his corps commanders, John B. Gordon, Lee agreed that the choices remaining were either: "make terms with the enemy," or break out of Petersburg to strike for the south.[49] With chances for the former now nil, Lee, reluctantly and even irrationally pursued the latter. Planned by Gordon at Lee's request, a March 25 assault on the enemy entrenchments near Union Fort Stedman was tactically brilliant but strategically flawed. According to his only report of this action, Lee said that he was "induced to assume the offensive from the belief that the point assailed could be carried without much loss, and the hope that ... I could ... cause ... Gen[era]l Grant ... to curtail his lines, that upon the approach of Gen[era]l Sherman [from the south], I might be able to hold our position with a portion of the troops, and with a select body unite with Gen[era]l Johnston and give him battle."[50]

The assumptions made here are baffling, especially as Lee's own experiences in the field against Grant would have validated none of them. Sherman was 150 miles away and not moving (and wouldn't until April 10); and Grant, now heavily reinforced by veteran troops recalled from the Valley, could be counted upon to be anything but passive. There is something disturbingly surreal about this whole enterprise that smacks of desperation—a quality not usually associated with Lee's generalship. Even biographer Clifford Dowdey, one of Lee's most eloquent defenders, could only describe his support of Gordon's plan as "cloudy-minded."[51]

Gordon's failed assault on Fort Stedman cost Lee nearly 3,000 casualties. In its aftermath there were small but significant gains of position by the Federal troops along other portions of the Petersburg siege lines. One of those became the jumping-off point for the wedge assault of April 2 made by the Union Sixth Corps, which broke Lee's line west of Petersburg and resulted in the death of A. P. Hill. The loss of these works, compounded by Sheridan's defeat of Pickett at Five Forks on April 1, made Lee's position untenable. With less than twenty-four hours warning to the Davis government in Richmond, Lee ordered all the troops assigned to defend the two cities to begin a pre-arranged withdrawal, commencing late on April 2. It was during the frantic preparations for this movement that he was handed a note from Jefferson Davis asking for more time. His uncharacteristic response was to tear the paper into pieces with the comment, "I am sure I gave him sufficient notice."[52]

The Confederate retreat to Appomattox Court House has acquired the aspects of legend. The image persists of a small, ragged band of starving fighters valiantly fending off the Yankee hordes until they were at last cornered near the small Virginia county seat whose name has become synonymous with the end of the Civil War. Yet a thorough modern study made by historian Christopher M. Calkins of the Army of Northern Virginia's final campaign suggests that many of the story's standard elements are incorrect.

Calkins concludes that ample supplies were generally on hand in the spring of 1865. What was lacking, he contends, was an effective method of distributing them. Some of the blame here must lie with Lee, who, despite his oft-quoted protests to Richmond about supplies, took no effective steps to improve distribution. Confederate sources indicate that on the night of April 2 there were 300,000 rations in Richmond, 80,000 at Farmville, and 180,000 at Lynchburg.

The size of the force that Lee led from Petersburg and Richmond has also been the object of much speculation. Southern accounts, needing to emphasize a disparity in numbers, place the total between 25,000 and 35,000 men. Historian Calkins, factoring backward from the number known to have surrendered at Appomattox, adding those captured during the campaign (accounted for by Federal POW rolls), noting those killed or wounded, and tacking on a modest figure of 100 desertions per day of the retreat, arrives at a figure of approximately 58,000.

So it was not a small ragged band that left the Richmond-Petersburg trenches on April 2, and for the most part the various units were moving according to the scheme laid down several weeks earlier. What failed was the structure of command within this mass of men. While some units preserved discipline and morale, many others trudged along more by instinct than conviction. The heart of the Confederate cause had stopped beating long before its military and political brains acknowledged the fact.

Lee's presumed retreat strategy was to steal a day's march on the enemy so as to be able to turn south through Burkeville for an eventual link-up with Johnston's army. Yet it was Lee himself who spelled the doom of this plan when, on April 4, he made the fateful decision to halt at Amelia Court House to reprovision his army. The 24-hour stop accomplished none of the objectives he had intended. He was unable to draw enough provender from the region to supply his troops, and the squandered headstart was turned to advantage by the closely pursuing Federals, who were able to force him to veer off his southward course to the west.

Lee could foresee the inevitable endgame. One day after he had changed direction, and following a disastrous fight by his rear guard along Sailor's Creek (which cost Lee another 7,700 men), he told an emissary sent from Jefferson Davis, "A few more Sailor's Creeks and it will be over—ended—just as I have expected it would end from the first."[53]

Much of the combat of this last campaign was more reactive than planned. Lee exercised no direct control over any of the larger actions fought during the retreat—either at Sailor's Creek on April 6 or Cumberland Church on April 7—and the only battle he did order, outside Appomattox Court House on the morning of April 9, seems to have been recognized by him as futile even as he initiated it.

On the night of April 8 he met with his corps commanders Longstreet and Gordon (Ewell had been captured at Sailor's Creek), along with Fitzhugh Lee (commanding his cavalry), to plan the next day's effort. If the army was to have any chance at all of surviving another day, it would have to utilize roads running south out of Appomattox Court House. A Federal force of unknown size and composition barred the way. If the enemy was merely a cavalry vanguard then there was every prospect that the Confederate army could bully its way through, though it would have to abandon its supply train. If, however, there were sizable infantry units ahead, the prospects of a breakout were slim. It was a contentious meeting, with Gordon certain that he had infantry in his front, while Lee was equally insistent that it could not be so. He overrode any objections and ordered the morning attack.

The chronology of events on the morning of April 9 says much about Lee's state of mind. Gordon's effort began at around 5:00 A.M. with a series of skirmishing probes lasting for about two hours. The general advance commenced about 7:00 A.M., and by 9:00 A.M. Gordon had cleared the escape route for the rest of the army to follow. The fighting up to this point had all been against Yankee cavalry and horse artillery; infantry units from the Twenty-Fourth, Twenty-Fifth, and Fifth Corps were closing, but would not come into contact with Gordon's men until nearly 9:30 A.M. While all this was unfolding, Lee rode out through the lines of Longstreet's Corps (which constituted his rear guard) at about 8:30 A.M. in the hope of meeting with U. S. Grant to discuss "the restoration of peace," as Lee had proposed in an April 8 communication.[54]

He was met by a Federal courier bearing a note written by Grant earlier that morning that rejected the proffered agenda because, as the Federal explained, "I have no authority to treat on the subject of peace."[55] (Lee had tried, in his letter, to shift the subject from the surrender of the Army of Northern Virginia to a wider-ranging discussion aimed at a broad peace settlement. Why he chose this tactic, after predicting its failure during the Longstreet-Ord discussions in February, is an unanswered question.)

Upon receiving Grant's note declining any broad peace talks, Lee immediately moved the topic to capitulation. Turning to his staff officer, Charles Marshall, Lee said, "Well, write a letter to General Grant and ask him to meet me to deal with the question of the surrender of my army."[56] It was about this time that Gordon's men made contact with the approaching Federal infantry, effectively ending the breakout attempt.

The moving events that ensued at the McLean House are well-known. Much has been said about Lee's humanity in refusing to continue the struggle in a guerrilla-like fashion. In so acting, he was responding no differently than any of his peers did when presented with similar options. To the Southern officer class the prospect of widespread social disorder was far more terrifying than the shame of surrender. Joseph E. Johnston actually defied an order from Jefferson Davis to disperse his army and surrendered it instead for that very reason. Also rejecting the guerrilla option were Richard Taylor and Edmund Kirby Smith. Lee's action was quite in line with this way of thinking.

Throughout his active service in the Confederate military, Lee had drawn a rather firm line between his strict military duties and any broader responsibilities. On the day after he surrendered his army, he met with Grant at the latter's request. The substance of his meeting is best described by Grant himself:

"Lee said to me that the South was a big country and that we might have to march over it three or four times before the war entirely ended, but that we would now be able to do it as they could no longer resist us. He expressed it as his earnest hope, however, that we would not be called upon to cause more loss and sacrifice of life; but he could not foretell the result. I then suggested to General Lee that there was not a man in the Confederacy whose influence with the soldiery and the whole people was as great as his, and that if he would now advise the surrender of all the armies I had no doubt his advice would be followed with alacrity. But Lee said that he could not do that without consulting the President first. I knew there was no use to urge him to do anything against his idea of what was right."[57]

Eleven days after surrendering to Grant at Appomattox, and five after he had returned to a now-occupied Richmond, Lee wrote

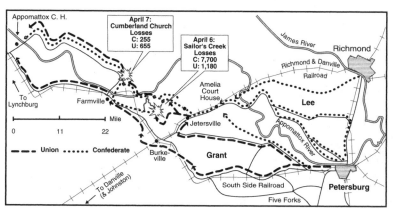

APPOMATTOX CAMPAIGN

Appomattox C. H.

April 7:
Cumberland Church
Losses
C: 255
U: 655

April 6:
Sailor's Creek
Losses
C: 7,700
U: 1,180

James River

Richmond

Richmond & Danville
Railroad

Amelia
Court
House

Lee

To
Lynchburg

Farmville

Appomattox River

Mile

0   11   22

Jetersville

Union ・・・・・・ **Confederate**

Burke-
ville

Grant

To Danville
(& Johnston)

South Side Railroad

Petersburg

Five Forks

Jefferson Davis a letter. After reviewing the sorry condition of his army at the start of its final campaign, and reflecting on the profound war-weariness that permeated the Confederacy, Lee ended with words he could never bring himself to say to Davis in person: "To save useless effusion of blood, I would recommend measures be taken for suspension of hostilities and the restoration of peace."[58]

CHAPTER 13

Finale

Lee departed Appomattox Court House on April 12, taking a measured pace that brought him to Richmond in three days. He found his way to the red brick house at 707 East Franklin Street, where his wife and two of his daughters were living. Everyone was safe but all had hair-raising stories of the long night thirteen days earlier when the capital had been evacuated by the Davis government and much of its downtown burned.

Among the blessings Lee counted was the survival of his immediate family. All three sons had served the South; Custis on President Davis's military staff, Fitzhugh as a cavalry officer ending the war with the rank of major general, and Robert Jr., with service first as an artilleryman, and later as staff officer. Daughters Mary, Agnes, and Mildred (none of whom would ever marry) spent the war with their mother or close by. Perhaps the worst for the experience was

Lee's wife, now wheelchair-bound and embittered. She told an acquaintance that the future "seems so dark now, that we are almost tempted to think God has forsaken us."[1] The loss of her beloved Arlington mansion remained an open wound that would never heal.

His first priority was to clarify his status as a paroled prisoner of war. He was in the process of doing this when he encountered one of Mosby's Rangers, still not yet surrendered. Asked if the unit should lay down its arms, Lee offered no opinion, citing his POW status as the reason. When the young man wanted to know what he personally should do, Lee had an answer. "Go home, all you boys who fought with me," he said, "and help build up the shattered fortunes of our old state."[2]

Lee wasn't in Richmond for two months when he learned that a Federal jury sitting in Norfolk had indicted him for treason. He wrote to U. S. Grant to confirm that the terms of the Appomattox surrender protected him and his men "from molestation so long as they conformed to its conditions."[3] Grant, who had crafted his provisions with an eye toward national reconciliation, answered in little more than a week. The Union general confirmed Lee's interpretation and indicated that the Federal government was dropping the proceedings. What he didn't say was that Andrew Johnson was so determined to make examples of prominent Rebels like Lee (whom he termed "an arch-traitor")[4] that only Grant's threat to resign his army post removed Lee's name from the President's enemies list.

As part of his personal reintegration into American society, Lee soon applied to have the rights and privileges of U.S. citizenship restored to him. When he learned that his application required a formal oath of allegiance, Lee dutifully made one on October 2, 1865. His signed and notarized statement reached the secretary of state's desk, where it was separately filed. This put Lee's earlier request to reconstitute his citizenship in limbo since the proof of his allegiance was not part of the paperwork. Lee would die with his case unresolved. It would not be settled until 1975 when the errant oath surfaced and was at long last mated with the application. Through an act of Congress signed into law on August 5, 1975 by President Gerald R. Ford, Robert E. Lee once more became a U.S. citizen.

Lee fully expected such roadblocks and went on with his life. For a while it seemed as if he would undertake to author what would have undoubtedly been the most important book by a Southern Civil War participant. Just three months after he returned to Richmond, he was approached by a New York publisher named C. B. Richardson who wanted him to write a military history of the conflict. Richardson met in Richmond with the general, who counterproposed a history of the Army of Northern Virginia's campaigns, if only he could obtain subordinates' reports and other papers not then available to him. The eager publisher promised to help track down the material. The project went so far as Lee sending out a circular to his principal officers requesting copies of all pertinent documents in their possession.

Richardson actually came bearing two deals. The other was for Lee to edit a reprinting of Harry Lee's Revolutionary War memoir. This he did right away. The original project never happened because of a new opportunity that fully absorbed his time. Had Lee not been diverted, there is ample reason to believe that his narrative would have emphasized themes already present in his letters and conversations: namely, the enemy's numerical and material superiority, and the failing of several subordinates to carry out his orders.

What turned the memoir project into one of history's "what ifs" was a visit by a gentleman named John W. Brockenbrough, who brought Lee an invitation to become the next president of Washington College in Lexington, Virginia. Lee considered the matter for a while and consulted with a few associates. Then he wrote to the school trustees, beginning with an explanation of why hiring him would be a bad idea before continuing that if the offer was still on the table he would take the job. Lee began his new career that very fall.

He would remain the college's president to the end of his life. His starting salary was $1,500 per year, a sum that he would triple after only a short time in office. He proved an able administrator and thoughtful mentor to young men. Under his stewardship the school's enrollment grew and its finances improved. There were challenges aplenty, both professional and personal. Lee brought much the same skill set to this task as he did when he was West Point's superintendent, and if neither resulted in any landmark moments, it could also be said that both institutions were better for his tenure. There is no evidence that he ever regretted his decision.

Whatever his feelings about the national stage, Lee was a figure of some notoriety, well known to both north and south. This was the probable reason why, in early 1866, he was summoned to testify before a Joint Congressional Committee that was attempting to gauge the impact Reconstruction policies were having on the South. Lee deflected most of the questions put to him by explaining that he was cut off from much of what was happening and not well informed.

In their efforts to pin him down, the questioners posed a number of hypotheticals, one of which touched upon the matter of personal integrity. Lee's answer, while couched in broad terms, spoke to his case as well. Southerners, he responded, "look upon the action of the State, in withdrawing itself from the government of the United States, as carrying the individuals of the State along with it; that the State was responsible for the act, not the individual."[5] Lee stated that while he might have taken an oath of allegiance to the Confederacy, he had no specific recollection of having done so. He also disclaimed all knowledge of intentional mistreatment of prisoners held in Southern camps.

The Congressional inquisitors wondered how the South was managing with its newly emancipated black population. Lee had long had problems with the ownership part of slavery, but he was square in the center of the Southern mainstream by holding that emancipated African Americans had to remain in their places on the social ladder. Granting them the right to cast ballots would wreck havoc since the ex-slaves, in Lee's words, "cannot vote intelligently." He went on record preferring a process of "gradual emancipation" and expressed his fear that a Constitutional amendment guaranteeing black suffrage would "excite unfriendly feelings between the races."[6]

(Not mentioned by the committee members present was the occasion in the war's final months when Lee lent his name to a plan that added armed slaves to the ranks of the Confederacy's armies. Reasoning that Federal black enlistments were siphoning off more and more of the slave manpower pool, Lee saw no reason why the Confederacy shouldn't draw from it as well. A company of black soldier "volunteers" was actually organized in Richmond and briefly served under his overall command during the Appomattox campaign.)

Lee's opinions about the battles he fought were much solicited but he studiously avoided any public forum where he might have to comment on the subject. In private, however, and in the company of a few trusted individuals, he spoke about some of the engagements he directed and decisions he made. While he had things to say about several of the major contests, the one that seemed to bother him most was Gettysburg. One gets the impression that Lee was still struggling to understand how that one got away from him.

Speaking about it with Washington College faculty member and former Army of Northern Virginia officer William Allen, Lee voiced his disappointment with Jeb Stuart, who "failed to give him information, and this deceived him into a general battle."[7] Conversing with a trusted cousin, Cassius Lee, Robert E. also had occasion to regret Ewell's hesitancy on July 1. "[Stonewall] Jackson," he said, "would have held the heights."[8]

Although Lee often protested that his only object now was to live peacefully out of the public eye, he was persuaded in winter of 1870 to tour the southern Atlantic coast. Ostensibly the trip was undertaken to bring him into a warmer climate where, it was hoped, his health (which had been failing) might be improved. Intended or not, it turned into a last hurrah for a man who found himself a certified American icon.

First stop was in Richmond, where he was visited by two officers who had served under him, John S. Mosby and George E. Pickett. Mosby, who had a private audience before joining with Pickett, thought that Lee seemed "pale and haggard," and that he "did not look like the Apollo I had known in the Army." Pickett's presence proved a mistake. He remained bitter about Gettysburg while Lee still hadn't forgotten his poor performance during the Virginia war's final campaign. Their meeting was coldly polite. Upon departing with Mosby, Pickett muttered, "He had my division slaughtered at Gettysburg." "Well," Mosby replied after some thought, "it made you immortal."[9]

Lee's journey continued with a sad stop in North Carolina, where he visited the grave of his daughter Anne. When he boarded the next train he was recognized by a telegraph operator who sent the news racing ahead that the great general was coming. A crowd gathered in Raleigh and chanted "Lee! Lee!" hoping for a glimpse of their idol. Surprised and not at all pleased by the demonstration, Lee refused to oblige and kept the curtains shut. But the outpouring of respect simply could not be ignored. At small stations or lonely crossroads they gathered, veterans with families and the curious, to wave or shrill the Rebel Yell. When Lee found he could not disembark for meal stops because of the crowds, food was brought to him by solicitous individuals.

The city of Columbia, South Carolina, declared a holiday in anticipation of his arrival, allowing the veterans to form ranks along the track, despite a heavy rain. This time, Lee emerged from his passenger car, raised his hat, and bowed to them. A stop over in Augusta was anything but the rest and relaxation Lee was seeking. There were lines of visitors to be greeted and lots of children, including a thirteen-year-old with a noteworthy future in store: His name was Woodrow Wilson.

Finally Lee and his daughter reached the endpoint of their rail journey, Savannah, where as a young engineering officer he had helped build a fort to guard the coast. Things were better organized here, but still the crowds were overwhelming. When the multitude outside the house where he was staying threatened to give him no peace, Lee's anxious host slipped his guest out an unobserved back door and settled him for the night with a neighbor.

The next leg of this odyssey was by steamer to Florida. Along the way a stop was made at Cumberland Island off the Georgia coast so that Lee could visit his father's grave. Although he wrote of the incident to his brother, Carter, he shared none of his thoughts at that moment. There was another halt at Jacksonville, where so many veterans lined up to pay him honor that he couldn't greet them all. Instead he faced them from the steamer's deck and acknowledged their salute. The journey's outward leg ended at Palatka, where he was the guest of his old commissary chief and enjoyed the experience of picking oranges from trees.

The return trip was no less eventful. At Charleston, South Carolina, there was a parade in his honor by the town's fire companies. Outside Wilmington, North Carolina, Lee shifted to a special train to carry him into the city. Waiting for him on the platform was a formation of cadets from the nearby Cape Fear Academy; they presented arms while ceremonial drums rolled. The citizens of Portsmouth, Virginia, did the Tarheels one better, greeting Lee with an antique field piece that roared its salute while fireworks exploded overhead. Then there were stops at various James River plantations, where his august presence awed at least one young lady present. "We had heard of God," she remarked later, "but here was General Lee!"[10]

Four days were spent in Richmond, where a doctor was consulted and the gentle measurings of a sculptor endured for a planned bust. Finally, two months and four days after leaving Washington College, Lee returned to what was now his home. Although the expedition had been undertaken in the hope it would aid in his recuperation, Lee himself said right afterward that "I do not think traveling in this way procures me much quiet and repose."[11]

Only a few months remained to him. There was time for school business, visits to not-too-distant localities, another sitting for that Richmond sculptor, and further consultations about his slowly worsening condition. Then Lee caught a cold on September 28, 1870, triggering an attack that left him speechless. Days passed and while he regained some of his voice, his words were hesitant, his sentences broken. There was a brief rally, then a steady decline until, not long after 9:00 A.M. on October 12, Robert E. Lee died.

Biographers eager to conclude his life's tale with a sterling epithet ascribe to him the final words: "Strike the tent." A more objective analysis of the symptoms (most likely a stroke), which caused him great trouble putting his thoughts into words, suggests that such a statement was apocryphal. In a way, that a warrior born who rose to prominence during this nation's most tumultuous period should die in a peaceful silence surrounded by his family was sufficient closure for the man and his legacy.

<hr/>

For nearly a century after his death, Robert Edward Lee was lost to American history. In his place was something the poet Stephen Vincent Benet termed the "marble man," a symbolic figure idealized and purified to the point where comparisons to Christ were common. If anything, his military accomplishments were elevated to an even higher plane. No less a world figure than Winston

Churchill would write of Lee as "one of the noblest Americans who ever lived, and one of the greatest captains known to the annals of war."[12]

In the one hundred years following his passing, Lee was the general who could do no wrong. Time and again he had triumphed against impossible odds, and if only those entrusted with his orders had been half as good and the enemy not so bountifully supplied, the story of the United States in the 1860s would have had a very different ending. Then the assassinations of Kennedy and King, the Vietnam quagmire, and the dark Nixon years unleashed a deeply skeptical historical wind that even scoured the marble man. A new Lee emerged, an ambitious Virginia-first racist prone to mistakes, who was recklessly profligate with precious white Southern lives. The costly aggressive course he pursued virtually bled out the Confederacy and guaranteed a Northern victory.

The image of Robert E. Lee in the twenty-first century is far less marble and much more man. A fresh generation of able biographers have kicked away the lofty pedestal, leaving us with a decidedly more complex, often contradictory, and ultimately more impressive portrait of an American whose life altered the nation's course, if only for a few turbulent years. In a similar fashion, measuring his prowess as a military commander is now blessedly free of the distortions inflicted by a century of hagiography.

What then can be said of General Robert E. Lee? At the top of the list, and too often overlooked, is the fact that he was a consummate professional. His pre–Civil War experience had been wide-ranging and his knowledge base was as good as anyone's in 1861. This in itself is no promise of greatness, since the roster of Civil War generals contains many intellectuals whose reputations pale when compared to Lee's.

Also rarely registered in any assessment was his ability to adapt to the dramatic changes taking place in the profession of arms. America's great general Washington never commanded more than

20,000 men. Lee at Gettysburg led over 70,000, his opponent even more. Everything connected with managing an army in the field was exponentially more complicated than ever before. While Lee's men would consistently suffer from logistical shortfalls, some of which can be ascribed to his modest management skills, Lee never lost his grip on the ultimate purpose of an army, which is to fight.

He was an adept strategic thinker who understood the myriad ways that events well removed from his immediate front could change the balance of power. Almost from the moment he took control of the Army of Northern Virginia, Lee grasped how linked he was to Confederate fortunes in the Shenandoah Valley. Successes there in 1862 made his victories before Richmond possible. Disasters there in 1864 were reverses that all the fortitude of the Rebel soldiers holding Richmond-Petersburg could not overcome.

Throughout the war, Lee demonstrated one absolutely necessary attribute for effective command leadership—self-confidence. This is a heaven-sent quality, not taught or learned but possessed. It served Lee well in the darkest moments at Chancellorsville, where an even momentary loss of nerve would have proven fatal. It misled him badly at Gettysburg, resulting in the spectacularly unsuccessful assault against Cemetery Ridge on July 3.

There were chinks in the armor as well. Whether he chose to ignore facts or was consistently uninformed by his staff, Lee could demand too much from his men and officers. To believe that the Army of Northern Virginia could be ready to fight again mere days after Sharpsburg was patently unrealistic. Additionally, Lee's reluctance to closely monitor subordinates tasked with critical assignments led directly to breakdowns in executing orders central to his designs. There were also times when his reliance on a specific officer blinded him to other options. Stuart's ride around the Union army prior to Gettysburg left behind two able brigades that were kept busy with minor duties because Lee did not know the commanding officers. Lee blamed Stuart for causing him to

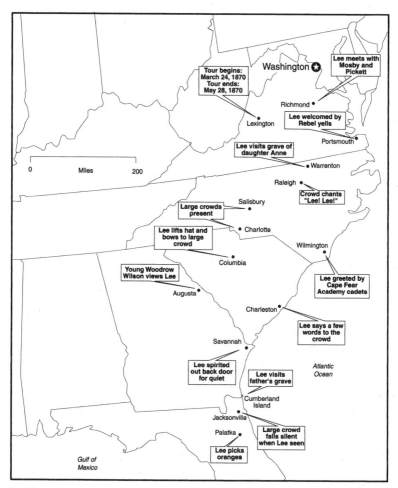

Tour begins:
March 24, 1870
Tour ends:
May 28, 1870

Lee meets with
Mosby and
Pickett

Washington ✪

Richmond •

Lee welcomed by
Rebel yells

Lexington •

Portsmouth •

Lee visits grave of
daughter Anne

Warrenton •

Raleigh •

Crowd chants
"Lee! Lee!"

Large crowds
present

Salisbury •

Lee lifts hat and
bows to large
crowd

Charlotte •

Wilmington •

Columbia •

Lee greeted by
Cape Fear
Academy cadets

Young Woodrow
Wilson views Lee

Augusta •

Charleston •

Lee says a few
words to the
crowd

Savannah •

Atlantic
Ocean

Lee spirited
out back door
for quiet

Lee visits
father's grave

Cumberland
Island

Jacksonville •

Palatka •

Large crowd
falls silent
when Lee seen

Lee picks
oranges

Gulf of
Mexico

0   Miles   200

LEE'S "FAREWELL" TOUR

stumble blind into battle at Gettysburg when he really had no one to blame but himself.

His command decisions, from the Seven Days through Gettysburg, are best understood as a determined quest for the battle of annihilation that would shock the enemy into talking peace. This put him at odds with Confederate President Jefferson Davis, who believed that just fending off the Yankee aggressors would be sufficient for iron-willed Southerners to outlast a weaker Northern determination. Sooner or later, Davis saw the North throwing up its hands in the face of stalwart Confederate resolve to protect its territory. Here, Lee's ability to build a bond of trust with his civilian commander-in-chief enabled him to undertake bold campaigns sanctioned with a free hand that few, if any, of his peers ever enjoyed.

Thanks to his unwavering focus on smashing the enemy, Lee was prepared to take great risks to achieve his ends. While his opponents habitually held back strength to insure against a total disaster, Lee would not hesitate to commit every man to the fight. Ascribing this to the numerical disparity he faced only partially explains this attitude. Other Southern generals, also confronting steep odds, found ways to preserve viable reserves. Lee, his sight set on the endgame of a total victory, accepted short-term risk for long-term gain. That such a course would be far more dear in the near-term was understood by Lee, who felt the losses but never regretted the decisions.

His sincere offer to resign after Gettysburg signals a struggle within his soul. Knowing now that he could not deliver the deciding victory, Lee needed to redefine his goals and objectives. No military leader of any consequence fights without some overriding purpose that allows him to accept the deaths and injuries his orders cause. To think that Lee just soldiered on after Gettysburg is to diminish the man. He found a new purpose: to use all his skills and the fighting spirit of his army to "upset the designs of the enemy" and to dissipate their plans. This would buy time for a political process to shape the peace he could not fashion through force of arms.

This was Lee's guiding star for the grueling campaigns of 1864. Even as he suffered through a series of debilitating health problems, he deftly parried enemy efforts to crush his army as he had once hoped to destroy theirs. In the period leading up to Gettysburg Lee also benefited from facing a series of Union commanders who simply were not in his class. McClellan, Burnside, and Hooker were psychologically defeated even before they joined battle. In the telling words of one Federal officer's assessment of Joe Hooker: "He knows that Lee is his master."[13] The advent of Grant changed everything. Grant refused to accord Lee all the powers others had given him and managed his operations in this spirit. Sometimes Grant underestimated Lee's abilities and then his men paid a terrible price, but in the long view Grant did prevail.

It was in the early months of 1865 that Lee came to understand that the war would not end through a political settlement. The near fanatic unwillingness of Jefferson Davis to consider any resolution short of total independence allowed no space for compromise. While Davis seemed to truly believe that there would be a rebirth of Southern nationalism in the eleventh hour, Lee saw with painful clarity that "the legitimate military consequences of [the enemy's numerical and material] . . . superiority have been postponed longer than we had reason to anticipate." Examining the critical decisions he made after abandoning Richmond and Petersburg, one is left with the image of a profoundly weary warrior crafting an honorable release for himself and his men.

Robert E. Lee never wrote a set of military maxims. An 1852 letter to son Custis comes as close as we can get to a philosophical summation of the man:

Live in the world you inhabit. Look upon things as they are. Take them as you find them. Make the best of them. . . . Do not imagine things are to happen as you wish. Wish them to happen right. Then strive hard to make them so. . . . Sad thoughts I know will sometimes come over us. They are necessary and good for us. They cause us to reflect. They are the shadows to our picture.[14]

Acknowledgments

One of the well-kept secrets of the National Park System is the number of fine historians based at its major historical sites. I asked several to look over sections of this book relating to their areas of expertise and all cheerfully complied. I'm grateful for the insights provided and critical notes given, and it's my pleasure to publicly acknowledge that assistance here:

Richmond National Battlefield Park: Robert E. L. Krick
   and Mike Andrus (Seven Days)
Fredericksburg & Spotsylvania National Military Park:
   John Hennessy (Second Manassas)
Antietam National Battlefield: Ted Alexander
   (Sharpsburg/Antietam)
Fredericksburg & Spotsylvania National Military Park:
   Donald C. Pfanz (Fredericksburg/Chancellorsville)

Of course, it's one thing to receive good advice and another to take it, and while I did in most cases, a few times we agreed to disagree. All conclusions and summaries are my own.

I also want to acknowledge that three chapters are drawn from previous work I've done: chapters 10 and 11 utilize research that I gathered for my book *Gettysburg: A Testing of Courage* (Harper-Collins, 2002), and chapter 12 similarly draws from research done for my essay "'A Mere Question of Time': Robert E. Lee from the Wilderness to Appomattox Court House" that originally appeared in *Lee the Soldier* (edited by Gary W. Gallagher, University of Nebraska Press, 1996).

Notes

Introduction

1. Douglas Southall Freeman, *R.E. Lee: A Biography* (New York: Charles Scribner's Sons, 1934–35), 4:121.
2. Edward Porter Alexander, *Military Memoirs of a Confederate* (1907; reprint, with a new introduction by Gary W. Gallagher, New York: Da Capo Press, 1993), 606.
3. James Longstreet, *From Manassas to Appomattox* (1896; reprint, Secaucus, NJ: Blue and Grey Press, 1984), 625.
4. Freeman, *R.E. Lee,* 4:120.

Chapter 1

1. Clifford Dowdey, *Lee* (1965; reprint, New York: Bonanza Books, n.d.), 36.
2. Dowdey, *Lee,* 41.
3. Emory M. Thomas, *Robert E. Lee: A Biography* (New York: W. W. Norton & Company, 1995), 42.
4. Both quotes are from Freeman, *R.E. Lee,* 1:41–42.
5. Freeman, *R.E. Lee,* 1:44.

Chapter 2

1. Freeman, *R.E. Lee,* 1:63.
2. Jacob Kobrick, "No Army Inspired: The Failure of Nationalism at Antebellum West Point," *Hi Concept, an Interdisciplinary Journal of Graduate Studies* (2004), 15.
3. A. L. Long, *Memoirs of Robert E. Lee* (1886; reprint, Secaucus, NJ: Blue and Grey Press, 1983), 30.
4. Thomas, *Robert E. Lee,* 55.

Chapter 3

1. Freeman, *R.E. Lee*, 1:47.
2. Elizabeth Brown Pryor, *Reading the Man: A Portrait of Robert E. Lee Through His Private Letters* (New York: Viking, 2007), 77.
3. Stanley F. Horn, ed., *The Robert E. Lee Reader* (1949; reprint, Old Saybrook, CT: Konecky & Konecky, n.d.), 69.
4. Thomas, *Robert E. Lee*, 120.
5. Freeman, *R.E. Lee*, 1:362.
6. Thomas L. Connelly, *The Marble Man: Robert E. Lee and His Image in American Society* (Baton Rouge, LA: Louisiana State University Press, 1977), 170.
7. Connelly, *The Marble Man*, 174–75.

Chapter 4

1. Thomas, *Robert E. Lee*, 116.
2. Freeman, *R.E. Lee*, 1:213.
3. Freeman, *R.E. Lee*, 1:229.
4. Freeman, *R.E. Lee*, 1:246.
5. Freeman, *R.E. Lee*, 1:247–48.
6. John S. D. Eisenhower, *So Far from God: The U.S. War with Mexico, 1846–1848* (New York: Random House, 1989), 311.
7. Eisenhower, *So Far from God*, 319.
8. Freeman, *R.E. Lee*, 1:258.
9. Freeman, *R.E. Lee*, 1:272.

Chapter 5

1. Robert E. Lee, Jr., *Recollections and Letters of General Robert E. Lee* (New York: Doubleday, Page & Co., 1904), 3–4.
2. Alan T. Nolan, *Lee Considered: General Robert E. Lee and Civil War History* (Chapel Hill, NC: The University of North Carolina Press, 1991), 11–12.
3. Nolan, *Lee Considered*, 10.
4. Freeman, *R.E. Lee*, 1:437.
5. Thomas, *Robert E. Lee*, 173.
6. Nolan, *Lee Considered*, 48.

Chapter 6

1. Freeman, *R.E. Lee*, 1:468.
2. Thomas, *Robert E. Lee*, 196.
3. Freeman, *R.E. Lee*, 1:475.
4. Dowdey, *Lee*, 160.
5. Dowdey, *Lee*, 160.
6. Thomas, *Robert E. Lee*, 201.

7. Thomas, *Robert E. Lee*, 209.
8. Thomas, *Robert E. Lee*, 212.
9. Freeman, *R.E. Lee*, 1:614.
10. Dowdey, *Lee*, 160.
11. Thomas, *Robert E. Lee*, 223.

Chapter 7

1. Long, *Memoirs of Robert E. Lee*, 168.
2. Freeman, *R.E. Lee*, 2:89.
3. Stephen W. Sears, *To the Gates of Richmond: The Peninsula Campaign* (New York: Ticknor & Fields, 1992), 155.
4. Gary W. Gallagher, ed., *Fighting for the Confederacy: The Personal Recollections of General Edward Porter Alexander* (Chapel Hill, NC: The University of North Carolina Press, 1989), 91.
5. Sears, *To the Gates of Richmond*, 174.
6. Thomas, *Robert E. Lee*, 234–35.
7. Clifford Dowdey, and Louis H. Manarin, eds., *The Wartime Papers of R.E. Lee* (New York: Bramhall House, 1961), 201.
8. Sears, *To the Gates of Richmond*, 200–1.
9. Sears, *To the Gates of Richmond*, 204.
10. J. B. M., "How the Seven Days' Battle Around Richmond Began" *Southern Historical Society Papers* 28 (January–December 1900), 95.
11. Sears, *To the Gates of Richmond*, 235.
12. Dowdey and Manarin, *The Wartime Papers of R.E. Lee*, 202.
13. Joseph P. Cullen, *The Peninsula Campaign 1862* (New York: Bonanza Books, 1973), 128.
14. Dowdey and Manarin, *The Wartime Papers of R.E. Lee*, 205.
15. Sears, *To the Gates of Richmond*, 307.
16. Freeman, *R.E. Lee*, 2:202.
17. Sears, *To the Gates of Richmond*, 314.
18. Sears, *To the Gates of Richmond*, 335.
19. Dowdey and Manarin, *The Wartime Papers of R.E. Lee*, 221.
20. Dowdey and Manarin, *The Wartime Papers of R.E. Lee*, 230.

Chapter 8

1. Clifford Dowdey, *The Seven Days: The Emergence of Robert E. Lee* (1964; reprint, New York: The Fairfax Press, 1978), 140.
2. Freeman, *R.E. Lee*, 2:261.
3. John J. Hennessy, *Return to Bull Run: The Campaign and Battle of Second Manassas* (New York: Simon & Schuster, 1993), 12.
4. Dowdey and Manarin, eds., *The Wartime Papers of R.E. Lee*, 267.
5. Hennessy, *Return to Bull Run*, 226.
6. Dowdey and Manarin, *The Wartime Papers of R.E. Lee*, 268.
7. Dowdey and Manarin, *The Wartime Papers of R.E. Lee*, 292.
8. Dowdey and Manarin, *The Wartime Papers of R.E. Lee*, 292.

9. Dowdey and Manarin, *The Wartime Papers of R.E. Lee,* 293.
10. All quotations: Dowdey and Manarin, *The Wartime Papers of R.E. Lee,* 294.
11. All quotations: Dowdey and Manarin, *The Wartime Papers of R.E. Lee,* 295–96.
12. Dowdey and Manarin, *The Wartime Papers of R.E. Lee,* 296.
13. Stephen W. Sears, *Landscape Turned Red: The Battle of Antietam* (New York: Ticknor & Fields, 1983), 86.
14. Dowdey and Manarin, *The Wartime Papers of R.E. Lee,* 298.
15. U.S. War Department, *The War of the Rebellion: A Compilation of the Official Records of the Union and Confederate Armies* (Washington, DC: Government Printing Office, 1880–1901), series I, vol. 19, pt. 2, 507. Hereafter referred to as OR.
16. Dowdey and Manarin, *The Wartime Papers of R.E. Lee,* 301.
17. Horn, *The Robert E. Lee Reader,* 241.
18. Dowdey and Manarin, *The Wartime Papers of R.E. Lee,* 303.
19. Thomas, *Robert E. Lee,* 261.
20. William Allan, "'Memoranda of Conversations with General Robert E. Lee,'" in Gary W. Gallagher, ed., *Lee the Soldier* (Lincoln, NE: University of Nebraska Press, 1996), 8.
21. Thomas, *Robert E. Lee,* 263.
22. Sears, *Landscape Turned Red,* 297.

Chapter 9

1. Steven E. Woodworth, *Davis & Lee at War* (Lawrence, KS: University Press of Kansas, 1995), 196.
2. Sears, *Landscape Turned Red,* 340.
3. Freeman, *R.E. Lee,* 2:421.
4. Freeman, *R.E. Lee,* 2:428.
5. George C. Rable, *Fredericksburg! Fredericksburg!* (Chapel Hill, NC: The University of North Carolina Press, 2002), 91.
6. Dowdey, *Lee,* 330.
7. Thomas, *Robert E. Lee,* 272.
8. Woodworth, *Davis & Lee at War,* 214.
9. Stephen W. Sears, *Chancellorsville* (New York: Houghton Mifflin Company, 1996), 44–45.
10. Thomas, *Robert E. Lee,* 272.
11. Allan, "Memoranda," in Gallagher, *Lee the Soldier,* 8.
12. Freeman, *R.E. Lee,* 2:481.
13. Freeman, *R.E. Lee,* 2:488.
14. Thomas, *Robert E. Lee,* 277.
15. Woodworth, *Davis & Lee at War,* 220.
16. Dowdey and Manarin, *The Wartime Papers of R.E. Lee,* 438.
17. Dowdey, *Lee,* 342.
18. Sears, *Chancellorsville,* 168.

19. Sears, *Chancellorsville*, 161.
20. Dowdey, *Lee*, 343.
21. Sears, *Chancellorsville*, 168.
22. Dowdey and Manarin, *The Wartime Papers of R.E. Lee*, 449.
23. Sears, *Chancellorsville*, 198.
24. Dowdey, *Lee*, 346.
25. Sears, *Chancellorsville*, 232.
26. Sears, *Chancellorsville*, 235.
27. Dowdey and Manarin, *The Wartime Papers of R.E. Lee*, 450.
28. Freeman, *R.E. Lee*, 2:528.
29. Dowdey and Manarin, *The Wartime Papers of R.E. Lee*, 465.
30. Sears, *Chancellorsville*, 307.
31. Freeman, *R.E. Lee*, 2:533.
32. Freeman, *R.E. Lee*, 2:534.
33. Dowdey and Manarin, *The Wartime Papers of R.E. Lee*, 451.
34. Thomas, *Robert E. Lee*, 286.
35. Sears, *Chancellorsville*, 386.
36. Freeman, *R.E. Lee*, 2:557.
37. Freeman, *R.E. Lee*, 2:562.
38. Thomas, *Robert E. Lee*, 287.
39. Horn, *The Robert E. Lee Reader*, 299.
40. Thomas, *Robert E. Lee*, 287.
41. Freeman, *R.E. Lee*, 2:560.

Chapter 10

1. Earl Schenck Miers, ed., *A Rebel War Clerk's Diary* (New York: A. S. Barnes & Company, Inc., 1961), 209.
2. *Columbus Daily Enquirer,* July 24, 1862.
3. OR, series I, vol. 25, pt. 2, 708–09.
4. Miers, *A Rebel War Clerk's Diary,* 210.
5. Henry Heth, "Letter to J. William Jones," *Southern Historical Society Papers* 4 (October 1877), 153.
6. Allan, "Memoranda," in Gallagher, *Lee the Soldier,* 17.
7. Miers, *A Rebel War Clerk's Diary,* 210.
8. Hudson Strode, *Jefferson Davis: Confederate President* (New York: Harcourt, Brace and Company, 1959), 405.
9. Frank Moore, ed., *The Rebellion Record: A Diary of American Events* (1861–1866; reprint, New York: Arno Press, 1977), vol. 6, 597.
10. Heth, "Letter to J. William Jones," 154.
11. Allan, "Memoranda," in Gallagher, *Lee the Soldier,* 17.
12. "A Lady of Virginia," *Diary of a Southern Refugee* (New York: E. J. Hale & Son, 1868), 214.
13. Thomas, *Robert E. Lee,* 289.
14. Donald C. Pfanz, *Richard S. Ewell: A Soldier's Life* (Chapel Hill, NC: The University of North Carolina Press, 1998), 273.
15. Allan, "Memoranda," in Gallagher, *Lee the Soldier,* 11.

16. William W. Hassler, *A.P. Hill: Lee's Forgotten General* (Chapel Hill, NC: The University of North Carolina Press, 1957), 142–43.

17. Lee complaints: Dowdey and Manarin, *The Wartime Papers of R.E. Lee*, 496, 500.

18. James Longstreet, "Lee's Invasion of Pennsylvania," in Clarence C. Buel and Robert U. Johnson, eds., *Battles and Leaders of the Civil War* (New York: Century Company, 1884–89), 3:249.

19. OR, series I, vol. 27, pt. 2, 848–49.

20. Lee quotations: Dowdey and Manarin, *The Wartime Papers of R.E. Lee*, 508–09.

21. OR, series I, vol. 27, pt. 3, 905.

22. Isaac R. Trimble, "The Battle and Campaign of Gettysburg," *Southern Historical Society Papers* 26 (January–December 1898), 121.

23. Dowdey and Manarin, *The Wartime Papers of R.E. Lee*, 524.

24. Francis W. Dawson, *Reminiscences of Confederate Service* (1882; reprint, edited by Bell I. Wiley, Baton Rouge, LA: Louisiana State University Press, 1980), 90–91.

25. John B. Hood, *Advance and Retreat* (1880; reprint, Secaucus, NJ: Blue and Grey Press, 1985), 54.

26. OR, series I, vol. 27, pt. 3, 931–32.

27. OR, series I, vol. 27, pt. 3, 942–43.

28. OR, series I, vol. 27, pt. 2, 848–49.

29. Trimble, "Battle and Campaign," 121–22.

30. James Power Smith, "General Lee at Gettysburg," *Southern Historical Society Papers* 33 (January–December 1905), 139.

31. Douglas Southall Freeman, *Lee's Lieutenants* (New York: Charles Scribner's Sons, 1944), 3:64.

32. Hood, *Advance and Retreat*, 55.

Chapter 11

1. Robert Pooler Myers, "Campaign from Culpeper C.H. Va. to Gettysburg, Pennsylvania," Eleanor S. Brockenbrough Library, Museum of the Confederacy.

2. Long, *Memoirs of Robert E. Lee*, 275.

3. Long, *Memoirs of Robert E. Lee*, 275.

4. Longstreet, *From Manassas to Appomattox*, 357.

5. Heth, "Letter to J. William Jones," 158.

6. James L. Morrison, ed., *The Memoirs of Henry Heth* (Westport, CT: Greenwood Press, 1974), 175.

7. James I. Robertson, ed., *Four Years with General Lee* (New York: Bonanza Books, 1962), 190.

8. Walter Clark, ed., *Histories of the Several Regiments and Battalions from North Carolina in the Great War 1861–'65* (1901; reprint, Wendell, NC: Broadfoot's Bookmark, 1982), 5:121.

9. Long, "Letter to General Early," *Southern Historical Society Papers* 4 (August 1877), 66–68.

10. James Longstreet, "Lee in Pennsylvania," in *The Annals of the War Written by Leading Participants North and South* (1876; reprint, Dayton, OH: Press of Morningside Bookshop, 1988), 420–22.

11. Smith, "General Lee at Gettysburg," 144.

12. Longstreet, "Lee in Pennsylvania," 420–22.

13. Long, "Letter to General Early," 66–68.

14. Jubal Early, "A Review by General Early," *Southern Historical Society Papers* 4 (December 1877), 272.

15. Early, "A Review by General Early," 272.

16. OR, series I, vol. 27, pt. 2, 308.

17. William Stanley Hoole, ed., *Seven Months in Rebel States during the North American War 1863* (Tuscaloosa, AL: Confederate Publishing Company, 1958), 113.

18. Samuel R. Johnston, "Letters," Douglas Southall Freeman Papers, Library of Congress.

19. William Stanley Hoole, ed., *Lawley Covers the Confederacy* (Tuscaloosa, AL: Confederate Publishing Company, 1964), 206.

20. Hoole, *Seven Months in Rebel States,* 113.

21. Campbell Brown and Richard S. Ewell Papers, Tennessee State Library and Archives.

22. All quotations: Johnston, "Letters."

23. Hood, *Advance and Retreat,* 57.

24. All quotations: Lafayette McLaws, "Gettysburg," *Southern Historical Society Papers* 7 (February 1879), 68–69.

25. Trimble, "The Battle and Campaign of Gettysburg," 125.

26. R. Lindsay Walker, "A Letter from General R. Lindsay Walker," *Southern Historical Society Papers* 5 (April 1878), 181.

27. Longstreet, "Lee in Pennsylvania," 422.

28. OR, series I, vol. 27, pt. 2, 318.

29. Thomas, *Robert E. Lee,* 298.

30. Arthur J. L. Fremantle, *Three Months in the Southern States* (1864; reprint, Lincoln, NE: University of Nebraska Press, 1991), 259–60.

31. Fremantle, *Three Months in the Southern States,* 260.

32. Noah Andre Trudeau, *Gettysburg: A Testing in Courage* (New York: HarperCollins, 2002), 411.

33. OR, series I, vol. 27, pt. 2, 320.

34. OR, series I, vol. 27, pt. 2, 320.

35. Henry B. McClellan, *I Rode with Jeb Stuart* (1958; reprint, New York: Da Capo Press, 1994), 337.

36. Jacob Hoke, *The Great Invasion* (1887; reprint, New York: Thomas Yoseloff, 1959), 355.

37. OR, series I, vol. 27, pt. 2, 320.

38. The Lee-Longstreet exchange is based on several sources. Lee's material comes from OR, series I, vol. 27, pt. 2, 320, 359. Longstreet's comments are taken from: *From Manassas to Appomattox,* 386; "Lee in Pennsylvania," 429; and "Lee's Invasion," 342.

39. Reconstruction of the discussion comes from several sources. Longstreet's comments are taken from: *From Manassas to Appomattox*, 288; and "Lee in Pennsylvania," 429. Walter Taylor's quotations are from Robertson, *Four Years with General Lee*, 103–04. A. L. Long's words are in *Memoirs of Robert E. Lee*, 288.

40. OR, series I, vol. 27, pt. 2, 351.

41. *Waco Daily Times-Herald*, n.d.

42. William H. Swallow, "The Third Day at Gettysburg," *Southern Bivouac* 1 n.s. (February 1886), 564–65.

43. OR, series I, vol. 27, pt. 2, 320.

44. Gary Kross, "Pickett's Charge!" *Blue & Gray Magazine* 16 (1999), 40.

45. Fremantle, *Three Months in the Southern States*, 264–65.

46. George R. Stewart, *Pickett's Charge* (New York: Premier Books, 1963), 256.

47. *Supplement to the Official Records of the Union and Confederate Armies* (Wilmington, NC: Broadfoot Publishing Company, 1995), 5:315; *Richmond Times Dispatch*, May 6, 1906.

48. All quotations: Fremantle, *Three Months in the Southern States*, 267.

49. Freeman, *R.E. Lee*, 3:129.

50. John D. Imboden, "The Confederate Retreat from Gettysburg," in Clarence C. Buel and Robert U. Johnson, eds., *Battles and Leaders of the Civil War* (New York: Century Company, 1884–89), 3:508–10.

51. Dowdey and Manarin, *The Wartime Papers of R.E. Lee*, 538–39.

52. Albert Wallber, "From Gettysburg to Libby Prison," in *War Papers: Being Papers Read before the Commandery of the State of Wisconsin, Military Order of the Loyal Legion of the United States* (1914; reprint, Wilmington, NC: Broadfoot Publishing Company, 1993), 196.

53. Freeman, *R.E. Lee*, 3:136.

54. Richard Barksdale Harwell, ed., *Cities and Camps of the Confederate States* (Chicago: University of Illinois Press, 1997), 65.

55. Freeman, *R.E. Lee*, 3:136.

56. OR, series I, vol. 27, pt. 2, 309.

Chapter 12

1. Dowdey and Manarin, *The Wartime Papers of R.E. Lee*, 589–90.

2. OR, series I, vol. 29, pt. 2, 640.

3. Dowdey and Manarin, *The Wartime Papers of R.E. Lee*, 605.

4. Dowdey and Manarin, *The Wartime Papers of R.E. Lee*, 688, 690.

5. Dowdey and Manarin, *The Wartime Papers of R.E. Lee*, 667.

6. Long, *Memoirs of Robert E. Lee*, 327.

7. OR, series I, vol. 36, pt. 2, 948.

8. Campbell Brown, "Memoranda—Campaign of 1864," Tennessee State Library and Archives.

9. Edward Steere, *The Wilderness Campaign* (New York: Bonanza Books, 1960), 336.

10. G. Moxley Sorrel, *Memoirs of a Confederate Staff Officer* (New York: Neale Publishing Company, 1905), 244–45.
11. Dowdey and Manarin, *The Wartime Papers of R.E. Lee,* 724.
12. Thomas H. Carter, "Colonel Thomas H. Carter's Letter," *Southern Historical Society Papers* 21 (January–December 1893), 239.
13. Morrison, *The Memoirs of Henry Heth,* 186–87.
14. Brown, "Memoranda."
15. Freeman, *R.E. Lee,* 3:326–27.
16. Dowdey and Manarin, *The Wartime Papers of R.E. Lee,* 745–46.
17. Dowdey and Manarin, *The Wartime Papers of R.E. Lee,* 748.
18. Michael J. Miller, *Even to Hell Itself: The North Anna Campaign* (Lynchburg, VA: H.E. Howard, 1989), 92.
19. Charles S. Venable, "The Campaign from the Wilderness to Petersburg," *Southern Historical Society Papers* 14 (January–December 1886), 535.
20. Dowdey and Manarin, *The Wartime Papers of R.E. Lee,* 756.
21. Dowdey and Manarin, *The Wartime Papers of R.E. Lee,* 764.
22. Dowdey and Manarin, *The Wartime Papers of R.E. Lee,* 767.
23. Dowdey and Manarin, *The Wartime Papers of R.E. Lee,* 775.
24. Dowdey and Manarin, *The Wartime Papers of R.E. Lee,* 765.
25. OR, series I, vol. 36, pt. 3, 877–78.
26. J. William Jones, *Life and Letters of Robert Edward Lee, Soldier and Man* (New York: Neale Publishing Company, 1906), 40.
27. OR, series I, vol. 36, pt. 3, 878–79.
28. Eppa Hunton, *Autobiography of Eppa Hunton* (Richmond, VA: William Byrd Press, 1933), 113.
29. Alfred Roman, *Military Operations of General Beauregard in the War Between the States* (New York: Harper & Brothers, 1884), 2:247.
30. *New York Tribune,* June 28, 1864.
31. OR, series I, vol. 40, pt. 1, 799.
32. Venable, "The Campaign from the Wilderness to Petersburg," 540.
33. OR, series I, vol. 42, pt. 2, 1161.
34. Fitzhugh Lee, *General Lee* (New York: Appleton and Company, 1894), 337.
35. John C. Reed, "Journal," Alabama Department of Archives and History.
36. John Horn, *The Destruction of the Weldon Railroad* (Lynchburg, VA: H.E. Howard, 1991), 49–51.
37. Richard J. Sommers, *Richmond Redeemed: The Siege at Petersburg* (Garden City, NY: Doubleday, 1981), 422.
38. Dowdey and Manarin, *The Wartime Papers of R.E. Lee,* 847.
39. Sommers, *Richmond Redeemed,* 207.
40. Dowdey, *Lee,* 522.
41. OR, series II, vol. 7, 1010.
42. J. B. Polley, *Hood's Texas Brigade: Its Marches, Its Battles, Its Achievements* (New York: Neale Publishing Company, 1910), 272.

43. John Esten Cooke, *A Life of General Robert E. Lee* (New York: D. Appleton and Company, 1871), 436.
44. Dowdey and Manarin, *The Wartime Papers of R.E. Lee,* 911.
45. OR, series I, vol. 42, pt. 2, 802.
46. Robert M. T. Hunter, "The Peace Commission—Mr. Hunter's Reply," *Southern Historical Society Papers* 4 (December 1877), 308–09.
47. Dowdey and Manarin, *The Wartime Papers of R.E. Lee,* 886, 890.
48. Dowdey and Manarin, *The Wartime Papers of R.E. Lee,* 905, 913.
49. Woodworth, *Davis & Lee at War,* 315.
50. Dowdey and Manarin, *The Wartime Papers of R.E. Lee,* 917.
51. Dowdey, *Lee,* 532.
52. Dowdey, *Lee,* 544.
53. John S. Wise, *The End of an Era* (Boston: Houghton Mifflin, 1899), 429.
54. Dowdey and Manarin, *The Wartime Papers of R.E. Lee,* 932.
55. Ulysses S. Grant, *Personal Memoirs of U.S. Grant* (New York: Charles L. Webster & Company, 1885), 2:483.
56. Frederick Maurice, ed., *An Aide-De-Camp of Lee, Being the Papers of Colonel Charles Marshall, Sometime Aide-De-Camp, Military Secretary, and Assistant Adjutant General on the Staff of Robert E. Lee* (Boston: Little, Brown, 1927), 254.
57. Grant, *Personal Memoirs,* 2:497.
58. Dowdey and Manarin, *The Wartime Papers of R.E. Lee,* 939.

Chapter 13

1. Pryor, *Reading the Man,* 433.
2. Dowdey, *Lee,* 595.
3. Thomas, *Robert E. Lee,* 370.
4. Jean Edward Smith, *Grant* (New York: Simon & Schuster, 2001), 418.
5. *Report of the Joint Committee on Reconstruction at the First Session Thirty-Ninth Congress* (1866; reprint, Westport, CT: Negro Universities Press, 1969), 133.
6. *Report of the Joint Committee,* 134–36.
7. Allan, "Memoranda," 18.
8. Freeman, *R.E. Lee,* 4:475.
9. Charles Bracelen Flood, *Lee: The Last Years* (Boston: Houghton, Mifflin Company, 1981), 232.
10. Freeman, *R.E. Lee,* 4:460.
11. Freeman, *R.E. Lee,* 4:465.
12. Gary W. Gallagher, introduction to *Lee the Soldier* (Lincoln, NE: University of Nebraska Press, 1996), xxi.
13. Michael C. C. Adams, *Our Masters the Rebels: A Speculation on Union Military Failure in the East, 1861–1865* (Cambridge, MA: Harvard University Press, 1978), 144.
14. Pryor, *Reading the Man,* 251.

Index

convention, 39–40 *See* West
Virginia
Virginia troops, artillery (1st Rockbridge
Battery, 63, 85) (Marmaduke
Johnson's Jackson Artillery, 61)
Virginia Central Railroad, 70
Virginia Military Institute, 40–1, 102
Virginia Peninsula, 2, 16, 46–7

Walker, John G., 78
Walker, R. Lindsay, 143
Wallace, Lew A., 185
War of 1812, 11
Warren, Gouverneur K., 173, 177
Washington, D.C., 76
Washington, George, viii, 12, 46
Washington, Martha, 18
Washington College, 203–4, 208

Weldon Railroad, battle, 183
West Virginia, 43–4, 121
Whistler, James McNeill, 32
White House, Va., 54, 63, 177–8
White Oak Swamp, battle, 64
White's Ford, 77
Whiting, William H. C., 62
Wilbourn, Robert E., 106
Wilcox, Cadmus, 183
Wilderness, battle, 165–7, 176
Williams, "Markie," 18
Williamsport, Pa., 87
Wilson, Woodrow, 207
Winchester, Va., 49, 188; battle, 120
Wool, John E., 19–20

yellow fever, 22
Yellow Tavern, Va., battle, 174